THE MAHARAL OF PRAGUE

The Story of Rabbi Yehudah Loew

THE MAHARAL OF PRAGUE

The Story of Rabbi Yehudah Loew

by
Yaakov Dovid Shulman

Copyright © 1992

All rights reserved.
This book, or any part thereof,
may not be reproduced in any
form whatsoever without the express
written permission of the copyright holder.

Published and distributed
in the U.S., Canada and overseas by
C.I.S. Publishers and Distributors
180 Park Avenue, Lakewood, New Jersey 08701
(908) 905-3000 Fax: (908) 367-6666

Distributed in Israel by
C.I.S. International (Israel)
Rechov Mishkalov 18
Har Nof, Jerusalem
Tel: 02-518-935

Distributed in the U.K. and Europe by
C.I.S. International (U.K.)
89 Craven Park Road
London N15 6AH, England
Tel: 81-809-3723

Book and cover design: Deenee Cohen
Typography: Nechamie Miller
Cover illustration: Gregg Hinlicky

ISBN 1-56062-168-0 hard cover
1-56062-169-9 soft cover
Library of Congress Catalog Card Number
92-73906

PRINTED IN THE UNITED STATES OF AMERICA

**DEDICATED TO
MY PARENTS**

Table of Contents

   Preface 13
1 The Four-Fold Blessing 15
2 Protector from Birth 21
3 The Formative Years 27
4 A Loaf of Bread 32
5 Rabbi of Nikolsburg 39
6 The Family Circle 48
7 Farewell, Moravia 52

8	The Gem of Europe	57
9	A Lesson in Learning	64
10	King Rudolph II	75
11	First Fruits	83
12	Advocate of Peace	86
13	The Iron Face	95
14	Rebuke and Leadership	106
15	Fighting Slander	112
16	The Maharal on Trial	126
17	A Delayed Letter	134
18	Spring in the Air	139
19	The Magic Banquet	144
20	Rumors in Moravia	156
21	Three Hundred to One	163
22	The Rabbi and the King	169
23	Out of Prague	184
24	On the Road Again	189

25 Thaddeus and the Golem 193
26 Blossoming Thoughts 206
27 The Elder Years 213
28 The Message for Posterity 222
29 The Final Days 228
30 The Maharal's Legacy 235

Preface

THE NAME OF THE MAHARAL OF PRAGUE IS KNOWN TO VAST NUMbers of Jews today, centuries after his death. To Talmudic scholars he is the author of profound glosses and commentaries. To those interested in Jewish philosophy and ethics his writings are timeless classics. And to the "man in the street" the legends of his *golem* are unique and unforgettable; although it is far from certain whether he ever created a human form by Kabbalistic means, he certainly took unformed matter and brought out its spiritual essence.

The Maharal encompassed and mastered the entire Torah literature and familiarized himself with the culture and way of thinking of the Jew of his day. In his voluminous writings, he synthesized this knowledge and expressed the truths of Torah in a form that would be most relevant to his generation. His success was so complete that his writings to this day have been an inspiration for many Jews, among them leaders who have based their own manner of framing their Torah insights on the teachings of the Maharal.

The Maharal was very active in community work. He did much to improve social ethics, in particular in relation to *lashon hara*. He was a far-seeing educator who founded the *Chevros Mishnayos* that spread across Europe and lasted for hundreds of years, and in addition, his many ideas for educational reform struck deep chords in many people.

The Maharal was a giant in all areas of Torah. He was an acknowledged master of *Halachah*, who is quoted by such authorities as the Bach, Maharam of Lublin, Magen Avraham and Taz. He blazed a new path in the interpretation of *Aggadah*. He was a man of his time and above his time, a man whose far-seeing gaze saw all the way to the days of *Mashiach*.

A fascinating figure who overcame community dissensions to lead forcefully; a Jew who received the singular honor of an interview with the Emperor of Bohemia; a man whose Torah is an expression of the best in human character and the most illuminating in holy inspiration—this was the Maharal.

Sources for this popular biography include *Hamaharal Miprague, Tekufaso Vetoraso, Likutei Maharal, Hashkafas Olamah shel Hayahadus* and *Rudolf II and His World*.

Legends that have been recorded about the Maharal and incidents which have not been verified are retold in this work. However, we have been careful to indicate which incidents are not from reputable historical sources.

Since this is a dramatized biography, the historical material was embellished with dialogue and description which do not purport to be an exact recording of events. All the incidents recorded and the quotations of the Maharal's teachings are from authentic sources, usually cited in the text.

1

The Four-Fold Blessing

BETZALEL VORMSER WAS DEEPLY DISAPPOINTED.

He had been glad yesterday to see his brothers drive up the cobblestone streets of Worms, Germany, returning to their home. He had greeted them with tears in his eyes, hugged them and kissed them warmly. Their father, Rabbi Chaim Vormser, had also been grateful to see them back, and their mother had embraced them joyfully, praising how wonderful they looked and how adult they had become.

Only Betzalel's sister, who was already married and living in Cracow, was not with the family. She had just given birth to her first child, Aryeh Leib, and could not travel.

Soon after the family finished dinner, Rabbi Chaim sat down at the study table with his two sons, Yaakov and Helman. Betzalel sat down at the end of the table.

Rabbi Chaim's wife sat at a chair in the room and listened

proudly to her grown sons. It seemed like only yesterday that they had been born and had learned to toddle across the room. These were the boys whom she had cleaned, who had stumbled over their first *aleph-beis*. She had made their meals, mended their clothing. She had soothed them, nursed them through illnesses, rebuked their mischievousness. And then she had sent them away from home—how hard it had been to see them leave! She had worried so much for them; they needed her so much! Yet she knew that they had to grow up. And now they were back; tall, bearded young men, Torah scholars who had studied with the greatest rabbis in Poland.

Rabbi Chaim stroked his mustache. "So we will hear how you learned in the *beis midrash* of Rabbi Shlomo Luria," he said. "What is it that they call him?"

"The Maharshal," Yaakov volunteered.

"Oh, yes."

Rabbi Chaim opened a volume of the Talmud, swung it around so that it faced his sons, and pointed to a *Tosafos*.

Yaakov and Helman read the *Tosafos* together in a sing-song chant, and soon they were discussing it enthusiastically with their father.

But Betzalel remain silent, and sorrow filled his heart. Three years before, he and his two brothers had told their father that they wished to go to Poland and learn with the great Rabbi Shlomo Luria. Rabbi Chaim had said that only two could go. Yaakov and Helman had left, while Betzalel had remained at home with his parents. Betzalel had accepted this with good grace. It was the will of his father and the desire of Heaven.

But now as he listened to his brothers discuss the *Tosafos*, Betzalel realized that they were missing subtle points that were obvious to him. It became clear that although they had learned in one of the greatest *yeshivos* in Europe and he had had to remain behind in Worms, his mind had a native sharpness that they lacked. And now he felt crushed. Why had they merited to go learn, while he had been forced to remain behind in Germany?

Betzalel entered into the discussion. He made a sharp point, bringing a clever proof from a seemingly unrelated source. His argument was fresh and unexpected but, once stated, seemed obvious and irrefutable. When his brothers raised objections, Betzalel easily showed the errors in their logic.

Betzalel was so sharp, so eager to best his brothers, that the debate heated up. Yaakov and Helman replied vigorously to Betzalel's attack, and they began to gain the upper hand. Their years of training began to show. They brought proofs from texts that Betzalel had never seen or did not recall. They introduced some of the new forms of logic that they had learned in Rabbi Luria's *yeshivah*, to which Betzalel was unaccustomed. A few times, Betzalel launched a counterattack based on his mental acuity, and his brothers had to scramble to counter his offensive.

But in the end, the training of Betzalel's brothers told. They buttressed their interpretation of the *Tosafos* with proofs and arguments that Betzalel could no longer contradict, and he yielded to them the victory.

Rabbi Chaim had listened with delight to his sons' vigorous and brilliant excursus through the *Tosafos*. They were still young, but they were already formidable Torah scholars—especially Yaakov and Helman; he was sure that they would attain high rabbinical posts. As for Betzalel, the boy had a sharp head on his shoulders, that was for sure, but he lacked the training necessary to become an outstanding authority.

"Excellent!" Rabbi Chaim said. "I am very pleased with all three of you. Yaakov and Helman, you have fully justified your stay at Rabbi Luria's *yeshivah*. As for you, Betzalel, although your learning is somewhat rough, you more than held your own. Your brothers have the advantage over you in learning, but they cannot match your sharpness and your logic."

Betzalel could no longer keep his thoughts to himself.

"Oh father!" he burst out. "If you see that I am sharper than Yaakov and Helman, why did you send them to the *yeshivah* and keep me behind? I wanted to learn the Torah so much! Now I have to get married and raise a family. For the rest of my life, I will never have the opportunity to make myself what I could have been."

The room fell silent. What could anyone say? How could anyone give Betzalel back the gift of becoming a *gadol hador*, a leader of the generation?

Rabbi Chaim's face turned sad and tender. "How can I answer you, my son?" he said. "Only two of my sons could go to Poland, and I could not predict who the best students would be. But you know that the essence of learning Torah is bringing Torah down to one's students and children. The Torah that your children learn will be in your merit." Rabbi Chaim stood up and told Betzalel, "Stand."

When Betzalel got up, Rabbi Chaim put his hands on Betzalel's head, as though to bless him.

Seeing this, Rabbi Chaim's wife and his other two sons also stood. They knew that Rabbi Chaim was a holy man and that his blessings would come true.

"While your brothers went to Poland to learn Torah, you remained behind to help me and your mother—one of the greatest and most difficult *mitzvos* of our Torah. In the merit of your having fulfilled that *mitzvah*, may God cause four lights to come forth from you."

Rabbi Chaim leaned over and kissed Betzalel on the head.

"Thank you, father," murmured Betzalel.

After this, the years passed swiftly. Yaakov and Helman both attained high rabbinical positions. Yaakov in particular attained a great post, first becoming rabbi of Worms and,

THE MAHARAL

many years later, in 1550, Chief Rabbi of Germany.

Betzalel's nephew Aryeh Leib grew up and became a great and famous rabbi in Cracow.

In the meantime, Rabbi Chaim and his wife passed away.

Soon after Betzalel received his father's blessing, the non-Jewish population of Germany, and of Worms in particular, resumed their anti-Semitic attacks. "The heart of a man is evil from his youth," say the Proverbs, but it is an unusually vigorous persistence that has enabled the hatred of Jews to accompany not only the youth but also the maturity of the jealous neighbors.

Betzalel left Worms and came to Posen, Poland. Poland was at that time under the influence of humanist philosophy and of a king interested in the economic benefits that the Jews could bring with them. Thus, the Polish Jews were somewhat spared the anti-Semitism of the Church and the merchants and lower-class nobility in the cities who feared Jewish competition. In consequence, Poland was to enter its Golden Age.

Posen was a major center of Jewish refugees from Germany. At the time that Betzalel moved there, Posen had one hundred thirty four Jewish households and a total Jewish population of about three thousand. Although this seems very small today, in those days, this was a sizable concentration of Jews. But Posen had more than just a quantity of Jews. It had a large number of outstanding Torah scholars, and Posen became a center of Jewish learning. Meanwhile, Poland overall had a Jewish population of about fifty thousand.

Here Betzalel married, and just as his father had predicted, he had four sons, each of whom was great in Torah and fear of God.

The oldest son was Rabbi Chaim. Later to become a student of Rabbi Shachna of Lublin and a comrade and study partner of Rabbi Moshe Isserles (the Rema), Rabbi Chaim went on to become rabbi of Worms and the author of *Vikuach*

THE MAHARAL

Mayim Chaim and other works.

The second son was the most famous and perhaps the greatest. He was named after his great-grandfather, Rabbi Yehudah Loew (pronounced *Loh-weh*), who had been famous as a holy man. The elder Rabbi Yehudah Loew had come to Worms, Germany, from Prague, in what was then Bohemia and what is now called Czechoslovakia. Betzalel's son, the younger Rabbi Yehudah Loew, would eventually move back to Prague. Yehudah is compared in the *Chumash* to a lion, and Loew is the German for "lion." After he became famous, Rabbi Loew was known by many names. His great contemporary, Rabbi Yaffe ("the Levush") called him "the Ari" ("lion" in Hebrew—not to be confused with the Ari of Tzfas). In Germany, he was known as *"Der Hohe Rabbi Lev"*—the great Rabbi Loew. But the name by which he has come to be known is the Maharal of Prague. The name Maharal is an acronym for *Moreinu Harav Loew*—our teacher Rabbi Loew.

After the Maharal, the next brother was Rabbi Sinai, who eventually became *rosh yeshivah* in Prague and afterwards *av beis din* in Nikolsburg, Moravia. He was also noted for his knowledge of history, and he became a teacher of Rabbi David Gans, who was also a student of the Maharal. Rabbi David Gans is known for his pioneering work of Jewish history, *Tzemach David*.

The Maharal's youngest brother was Rabbi Shimshon, who became Chief Rabbi of Kremnitz, Poland.

2

Protector from Birth

YEHUDAH LOEW WAS BORN ON THE EVE OF *PESACH*, DURING THE first *seder* night. His birth was indeed to bring a redemption to the Jews of his time, and his influence continued to affect and inspire many individuals and leaders of Jewish thought in the centuries after his death. In his teachings, the Maharal brought the true, internal redemption of clarity of mind and the opening of consciousness. His vigorous leadership in Moravia, Posen and Prague would imbue generations with his sense of justice and goodness. His formulations on the way that God rules the universe and on how man serves God was the inspiration of the leaders of both Lithuanian and *chassidic* Jewry and, after them, of those who have blended the two.

Around the Maharal have grown many stories. In these legends, the Maharal was not only a community leader, not only a wise and holy man, not only a brilliant and magnificent thinker. He was also the Jews' protector against the anti-Semitic tormentor, and in particular against the odious charge of the blood libel, the calumny that Jews mixed the blood of Christian children into their *matzos* for *Pesach*.

This is the fondly-told story of the Maharal's birth, as it is usually recounted.

The table is covered with a white tablecloth; candles are shining; *matzos* and bottles of wine are upon the table; and the family sits about the table, reading from *Haggados*. But outside the house, in the dark of an unlit street, one can barely make out a disheveled, dirty peasant, bent under the weight of a distended sack. But why is he so furtively lurking along the sides of the houses? Why does he seem so eager to avoid the light that emanates from the Jews' houses, casting its feeble glow into the murky streets?

Rabbi Betzalel sat at the head of his table like a king. The candles flickered brightly, the table was richly set, and his family and guests reclined like guests at a regal banquet. They truly felt free, truly rulers in their own land, redeemed and living only under the yoke of Hashem. This was the night called *Leil Shimurim*, when God watches over the Jews, the night of freedom. Rabbi Betzalel recalled that he himself was a descendant of King David, and so might King David have sat at the royal table. And if it might be thought presumptuous to make such a comparison, did not the Talmud teach that all Jews are kings and sons of kings?

The gentile servants brought in the water for the celebrants to wash their hands and then the *karpas* vegetable. Betzalel often glanced at his wife, sitting with the women at the opposite end of the table. Whenever he caught her eye, she smiled and nodded, as if to say, Everything is all right. Even the table could not conceal the fact that any day, she and Betzalel would be the parents of a second child. Their firstborn, Chaim, barely old enough to lisp the Four Questions,

THE MAHARAL

was the delight of all his relatives at the table.

At the beginning of *Dayeinu*, Rabbi Betzalel's wife gasped. But when Rabbi Betzalel looked at her, she returned a reassuring smile.

Then another gasp. Then yet another.

The woman next to her patted her hand. "Is everything all right, my dear? Should we call for the midwife?"

"No, no, I'm not due for another week."

Rabbi Betzalel, who had stopped his reading in mid-verse, again resumed, and the company broke into a lively tune.

But his wife's time to deliver would come prematurely. Her unborn child had sensed the shadow of evil approaching, and he tossed back and forth within his little sphere of life. Something must be done! The Jews must be helped!

A stealthy figure skulked along the street, lugging a heavy sack. As he passed the open window of a family celebrating the *seder*, the candlelight fell momentarily upon his face; a sallow visage, gray, cruel eyes, a long nose and, under sensuous, coarse lips, a long and stubbly jaw. The peasant trudged past the house. He was interested only in the house of the rich Jew, Betzalel.

Hadn't the priest told them at church that the Jews were the enemies of mankind, that they had murdered the Christian savior and must forever suffer punishment? Hadn't the priest told them that at Easter time, when Christians recall the founder of their faith, they must recall those who caused him suffering and death? And now these Jews were swarming into the country, robbing the Christians of their gold and meat.

(He did not consider the Church's heavy taxes for its magnificent churches and the generous support of its many officers; he forgot the Christian moneylenders charging exorbitant interest on their loans and keeping debtors in hopeless servitude; and he did not think it was necessary to mention that Christian kings instigated rivalries that sent armies through the countryside, devastating farms.)

No, look at the rich Jews, squeezing the Christian dry of money, the Jews who poison the wells and intone evil spells that spoil the fields. Hadn't there been a dry spell recently that had ruined the barley crop? And hadn't the Jews been seen praying and dancing under the light of the new moon?

But the worst crime of all, the peasant recalled from the priest's diatribe, just as the Jews had murdered the Christian savior, so did they every year slaughter a Christian child, a pure, Christian child—here the peasant felt a thrill of horror and indignation—and knead its blood into their infernal unleavened bread for Passover!

The peasant crept closer to the home of Rabbi Betzalel. His hands trembled from exertion and passion. In the sack, he carried—he didn't want to think of it—his young son, his own son. He was so sorry that the boy had died. He knew that he had been wrong to beat him so hard—he knew it, he admitted it. He wasn't so hard-hearted as to deny that. But what could he do, when the boy had been so wicked and disrespectful? He had a right, didn't he, to discipline his own children? Didn't the Holy Book tell us that he who spares the rod spoils the child?

But perhaps he ought not to have clubbed him as hard as he had. Ah, well, it was out of his hands. At any rate, maybe now he would gain grace from Heaven, for with this son of his who had died—this heedless, wayward son—he could still redeem himself.

The peasant stopped at a corner and took a deep breath. Sweat glistened on his temples and hollow cheeks. Just down the street, he saw the bright window of Rabbi Betzalel's house. In only a few more minutes, he would deposit the body of the child in the courtyard. He would run to tell the magistrate that he had seen the servants of Betzalel, the rich Jew, bring a large sack into his courtyard.

THE MAHARAL

The peasant crawled along the sides of the houses, his head spinning. He was almost there—just one more house, and then he would just have to open the courtyard gate—

From the rich Jew's house, a woman screamed. There was a sudden commotion of Jews jumping up and calling out. A moment later, a group of Jews clattered down the steps and burst into the courtyard.

He had been seen! That confounded Jewish woman had caught sight of him! Cursing his bad luck, he swung around and started running down the street, hindered by the heavy sack that rolled across his back. Behind him, he heard footsteps and voices calling out in the unintelligible Jewish tongue. He had to get away, out of the Jewish ghetto, back to safety!

Behind him, the Jews called in the language that he didn't understand, "Quick, get the midwife, tell her to come immediately! Tell her Rabbi Betzalel's wife has started to give birth!"

The peasant ran frantically, but with the sack on his back, he could not outrace his pursuers. But at last he saw that he was coming to the Christian quarter. If he could only reach it, he would be among Christians, and then he would be safe.

The guard sitting at the entrance of the Jewish ghetto had leaned his chair back against the wall and dozed off to sleep.

Now the sound of running feet and raised voices woke him. He jerked up with a violent twitch that sent his chair skidding from under him, and he staggered to his feet, leaning desperately against the wall.

A peasant carrying a sack was being pursued by a pack of Jews dressed in their festive clothing. Oh ho, the guard thought, a little thievery that went sour! If he caught this thief, he would surely be in the magistrate's good graces.

As the peasant ran up to the ghetto entrance, the guard leaped out, waving his stick.

The peasant looked up at him. "The Jews!" he cried. "Help me—"

"Stop, thief!" the guard cried, and when the peasant barged right by him, he brought his stick heavily down on the peasant's shoulder.

The peasant staggered and fell. To the guard's amazement, the Jews didn't stop but ran right by them.

"That's right odd," the guard exclaimed. Looking down, he saw that the sack had slipped from the peasant's grip and fallen to the ground. And then the guard gave an exclamation, for extending from the opening of the sack was a dirty child's hand.

"Well, well, well," said the guard, reaching down and grabbing the peasant by the scruff of the neck. "I think you've got a bit of explaining to do, what?"

And so, even at the moment of his birth, the Maharal was the protector of his people.

3

The Formative Years

YOUNG YEHUDAH LOEW GREW UP IN AN ATMOSPHERE OF TORAH scholarship, piety and wealth. He had all he needed to grow to his highest potential: loving parents, his physical needs taken care of, and his brothers and comrades. He had the full use of his father's Torah library, and the opportunity to study in the most nurturing Torah environment that he could wish. And in addition, he had relatives in prominent rabbinical positions and some even in high governmental posts.

In the year of Yehudah Loew's birth, the famous printing firm Gershoni opened a printing press in Prague. This was the first printing press for *sefarim* of quality in all of Central Europe. This probably made it much easier than it would have been otherwise for Yehudah Loew to gain access to many important *sefarim*.

Yehudah Loew made full use of these opportunities. In his

later writings, we see the results of his long years of study and insight in all areas of Torah thought, as well as his exposure to the sciences and philosophies current in his day.

In his writings, the Maharal does not give the names of any of his teachers. Although he apparently studied under the Maharshal for a time, he does not mention him as his teacher. Nor does the Maharshal mention the Maharal as a student, although he does refer to him as "a lion of the Torah." In his writings about how to learn Torah, the Maharal did not stress learning under a teacher but rather learning in a group with colleagues. Besides this, even when the Maharal relies on the terms or ideas of other *sefarim*, he often does not mention them by name. He has so transformed their ideas that the concepts are original and his.

From this, it can be conjectured that as a young man, the Maharal learned mainly on his own and with comrades. In this way, he could follow the path of his own genius, unencumbered by external systems. The Maharal gained his knowledge through independent study, fueled by inspiration and grounded by self-discipline.

The institution in which the Maharal learned tended to reinforce this. The Polish *beis midrash*, unlike the *yeshivah* model, was based on the idea of independent study, in which students learned as a group.

The Maharal was fortunate that his father and teachers, loving and respecting him, were sensitive to his needs and appreciated that he was an individual who needed to blossom in his own way. They supported him while allowing him to follow his own path.

The Maharal grew up to be an expert in *Tanach* and its principal commentators: Rashi, Ramban, the Radak, Ibn Ezra and the Ralbag. In his later writings, the Maharal took issue with Ibn Ezra for disagreeing with statements in the Talmud and with the Ralbag for his rationalistic approach to miracles.

THE MAHARAL

The Maharal became an outstanding student of the Talmud. The prevailing study method of the day was the system of brilliant discourse entitled *pulpal*, *chidudim* or *chilukim*, and the Maharal became a master of this. In later years, however, he became a sharp critic of this method of Talmud learning and proposed his own educational methods.

The Maharal was also well-versed in Kabbalah, and in his writings, he mentions such works as the *Zohar*, the *Bahir*, *Osios d'Rabbi Akiva* and others.

The Maharal was also thoroughly familiar with the works of the Jewish philosophers, such as the Rambam, Crescas and Albo. He was also acquainted with Greek philosophy, physics, mathematics and astronomy.

In his later writings, the Maharal taught that secular learning cannot take a person to the core of truth—only the Torah can do that. But one can, the Maharal said, "learn anything whose purpose is to understand the essence of the world . . . for all of creation is the work of God, and one must recognize this and, through nature, recognize God." (*Nesivos Olam*) However, the Maharal cautioned, this should be learned not from non-pious individuals but only from books that do not contain heretical ideas.

The Maharal drew all learning together so that everything would serve to bring him close to God. He developed a style that used the terminology of philosophers to express the ideas of the Kabbalah. Other rabbis who followed him have utilized his method, to such an extent that those who study them sometimes believe that they are reading vaguely spiritual writings, rather than deep, Kabbalistic texts.

In this way the Maharal spent his youth and early adulthood.

The Maharal did not become a prominent community leader in his early years, as did, for instance, the Rema. Well into middle age, he was able to allocate much of his time for

THE MAHARAL

private study in preparation for the communal activities and Torah teaching still to come.

The years passed. The Maharal was immersed in the world of Torah and holiness. But into the sweet life of the *beis midrash* came occasional news of the occurrences of the outside world.

In 1523, Martin Luther, the German priest who had staged a one-man revolution against the Catholic Church and thus started the movement that would result in Protestantism, issued a pamphlet in which he attacked the Catholic Church for its persecution of the Jews. Jews were filled with elation at their new defender and were hopeful that he would bring about an end to Christian persecution.

Luther's spirit of openness to Judaism had an unexpected result. Rather than resulting in the conversion of Jews, his policy inspired some of his followers to turn to Jewish practices—in particular, to observe their Sabbath on Saturday, rather than Sunday.

Luther responded with wrath. In a 1538 tractate, the "Letter Against the Sabbathers," he declared of the Jews, "This people was possessed by all devils." And he denounced the Judaizing Protestants.

In 1542, Martin Luther published a long tractate, "The Jews and Their Lies," and he concluded, "What should we do with these contemptible, damned people, the Jews?" And he answered his own question, "First, their synagogues or schools should be set on fire. Second, their houses should also be totally destroyed, since they practice the same evil there as they do in their schools. Third, all their prayer books and Talmud books, which are full of idolatry, lies, curses and blasphemy should be taken away from them. Fourth, their rabbis should be forbidden on pain of death to teach. Finally, they should not be protected by the police. They should not be allowed to lend at interest. [Earlier, he had written, "If they

THE MAHARAL

are driven to lending on interest, how can they refrain from it?"] And all their money, gold and silver should be taken away from them, for everything they have was stolen from us."

Meanwhile, in 1529, the Turks had attacked Austria, beginning a bloody, decades-long war. The subsequent Turkish attack on Central Europe in 1542 opened an opportunity for anti-Semites. Prague had suffered many fires that year. The Jews were accused of setting those fires, as well as of sending secret war preparation plans to the Turks.

In consequence, all the Jews of Bohemia—including the Jews of Prague—were expelled from the country.

4

A Loaf of Bread

YEHUDAH LOEW WALKED SLOWLY TO THE BEIS MIDRASH, HIS MIND filled with exciting combinations of thoughts and concepts he had encountered, thoughts from the Talmud, from the Rambam, from the *Zohar* all revolved around each other in his mind and then began to resolve themselves into new, fresh ideas that spoke in the language of his generation.

With these thoughts occupying him and sweetly filling his mind, Yehudah Loew hardly paid attention to the street through which he walked or the stone stairs he climbed and the door he opened to the *beis midrash*.

"Yehudah!" a brash voice interrupted his reverie. The flashing grin of a short, young man in a long, rabbinic caftan pulled him back to this world.

"Daniel!" Yehudah Loew smiled. "You gave me a shock."

"It's a long trip from walking through seventh heaven to

learning a *blatt Gemara* here in Premsla."

"Maybe not so far," Yehudah said. "Are you ready to learn?"

"In just a few minutes, Yehudah. Some of us still need to eat breakfast." His bright teeth flashed. "But look at this." Daniel waved a thick letter before Yehudah Loew's eyes.

Yehudah Loew looked back questioningly at Daniel.

"It's a letter for you from your parents. But I suppose you're too busy floating in Heaven to read it?" Daniel smiled ironically.

"A letter from my parents! Let me have it, Daniel. I'll speak to you later."

Yehudah Loew took the thick letter and fingered the red sealing wax with great curiosity. He stepped into the courtyard, sat on a bench in the rays of the pale sun and tore open the paper.

Inside there were two letters. The first, a short note, read,

Dear Yehudah Loew,
    Your mother received the enclosed letter this morning from your fiancee Perl. Although matters still must be resolved, we thought you would want to read it immediately.
    Wishing you every good fortune, and hoping to rejoice at your wedding soon,
                        Your loving father and mother

Yehudah Loew took out the other letter and unfolded it. It was in Perl's neat and graceful handwriting. He began to read.

My dear mother-in-law,
    You and your worthy husband, my dear father-in-law, should soon be receiving a letter from my father, may he live long, regarding the great and wonderful changes that

have taken place in our lives, literally miracles, divine providence in a most revealed way! May God be praised and blessed.

But I could not hold myself back from taking pen in hand and writing you first and sharing the gladness of my heart with you, my dear mother-in-law, and telling you of all the gladness and joy that we have had.

I do not have to remind you of our sad state of affairs. You were at our house several years ago, and you saw the great comfort and splendor in which we lived, our large mansion, our many servants, our carriage and our horses. You recall that we had the finest delicacies for dinner, the finest dresses, and that musicians played at our festive occasions.

But this is vanity. You recall that my father had a wonderful *sefarim* library, that he gave charity freely to everyone who came to his door, as well as to all the organizations that support the poor. You recall that he hired many Jews who would otherwise not have had to eat.

And then, when my dear father and mother were growing old, God changed his fortunes, for the world is like a spinning wheel. For our sins, with the disruptions caused by the war with the Turks and all the particular details of which I do not have to remind you, my father lost his business and rapidly lost his wealth.

Not only did he lose his money, but the creditors seized our house and sold our silver, our furniture and even our pillows. We had to move to a small apartment and live on the small amount of money that was left us. My father and mother, may they live long, were so broken that they could no longer work.

It was then that my father, may he live long, wrote and said that because he could no longer fulfill his obligations, he would free your son, my betrothed, from the obligation of marrying me.

And your son, my betrothed, in his goodness and righteousness saved me from humiliation and sadness, and promised to uphold his promise to marry me despite my

THE MAHARAL

change in circumstances. May he be blessed a thousand times!

Yehudah Loew passed over this paragraph quickly. Perl was truly a fine daughter of Israel to be so appreciative of a simple act that any decent Jew would do. Then he read on.

> Then, as I believe you may know, dear mother-in-law, the burden of supporting myself and my dear parents, may they live long, fell on my shoulders.
> Below our small apartment, was a room with a baker's oven. We rented this, and I began baking bread. You can imagine that in those times no one had very much money, and so we barely made a living. But everyone needs bread, and so, thank the merciful God, we were able to live and support ourselves with dignity, and what more can we ask of God?
> But this year, the war with the Turks has caused ruin and desolation even in our part of Poland, may God have mercy.
> Soldiers ride across the countryside, taking food as they want, staying in whose quarters they will, stealing when they want to, going about drunk and violent, and everyone shivers and is in great fear of them.
> I will now tell you the wonderful miracle that God did for us, may He be blessed, and how He saved us and redeemed us from our poverty and pitiful circumstances.
> About six weeks ago, as I was carrying a basket of bread loaves through the street to bring them to the marketplace, a soldier rode right up to me on his horse, holding his sword in his hand. I grew very frightened and turned to run away, but before I could do so, he took his sword and thrust it through a loaf of bread from my basket.
> If I had been wiser, I would have fled and thanked God that the soldier had only wanted to steal this one loaf of bread and no further wickedness, may God protect us.
> But when I saw him stealing the food from the mouths

THE MAHARAL

of my father and mother, may they live long, I was filled with great anger and strength.

I grabbed his horse's bridle and hung on.

"Why do you steal my bread?" I said to him. "I am a poor girl, and my father and mother are too old to work, and I support them with this bread."

I looked up at the soldier. His face was pale and his eyes were not evil, as are the faces of most of the soldiers.

I am only a weak woman, and I burst into tears and begged the soldier to give me back the bread, for the lives of my parents depended on it.

God caused my words to touch the soldier's heart, and he answered me as follows: "I have not eaten for three days, if I do not have this bread, I will die. But take this pouch from my saddle. I will come back within twenty-four hours to pay you for the bread, and if I do not, you may keep whatever is in the pouch."

Then he gave me a cloth pouch. I let go of the bridle, and he rode away.

The soldier didn't come back, but for many days, I did not want to touch the pouch. But finally, after a month, I spoke about it with Rabbi Shimon Elazar, who said that I may open it and keep whatever I may find.

I went home and undid the pouch, with little hope of finding anything of worth. The pouch was quite heavy, but many things are heavy—copper coins, or stones. When I opened the tight knot of the pouch and looked in, imagine my joy and gratitude to God to see there a heap of shining coins! I poured them out onto the table and called my father and mother, may they live long. The coins were all of solid gold, and we rejoiced exceedingly and gave thanks to our Father in Heaven for His miraculous kindness.

And now, as a result of this mercy and kindness from Heaven, my father can again fulfill his obligations to your son, my betrothed, and he will himself be writing a more formal letter to you and to your son, my betrothed.

But I am just a simple woman—

THE MAHARAL

It is not just a simple woman, thought Yehudah Loew, who will even in terrible poverty not look into a pouch that she fears may not be hers.

> —and I wished to share this joy with you myself in my own few and simple words.
> And so I wish you every joy and happiness, and may the merciful God send you health and long life.
> Your loving daughter-in-law,
>
>   Perl

Yehuda Loew put down the letter, his heart singing with gladness. "Praised is Hashem!" he murmured. "Blessed be He who is good and who does good."

The heavy wooden door to the courtyard opened, and Daniel came out and, passing under the leaves of the linden tree that brushed his head, walked toward Yehudah Loew.

"Are you ready to learn?" Yehudah Loew asked.

Daniel grinned and waved an envelope. "You've got another letter. The return address is your fiancee's father." He handed the letter to Yehudah Loew and then added in a more sober tone, "Good news, I hope?"

Yehudah Loew tore open the letter and began to read:

Dear Yehudah Loew, may his light shine,
> With thanks and praises to the merciful God of heaven and earth, He who brings low and who raises up, I am filled with joy to be able to tell you that I have, through God's lovingkindness, with no merits of my own, been saved and redeemed, and my horn lifted up. With a revealed miracle—

Yehudah Loew stood up. "Good news, Daniel," he said. "The best kind of news. May God be praised."

"Whenever one thing desires its opposite," wrote the Maharal in later years, "the reason is that it is fulfilled by that opposite. Because it is fulfilled, the two become one. This is the cause of human love." (*Nesivos Olam*)

In 1544, the Maharal was married to Perl, daughter of Reb Shmuel, known as "Rich Shmelke." He was thirty-two years old, and she was twenty-eight.

In that year, the Jews who had been expelled from all of Bohemia, including Prague, were allowed to return home.

The Maharal lived together with his wife for the next sixty-six years. They had six daughters, one son, and numerous grandchildren and great-grandchildren, many of whom became important Torah figures and community leaders.

The Maharal's first daughter was Leah. Soon afterward, his second daughter, Feigeleh, entered the world.

In 1549, Rabbi Chaim, the Maharal's brother, opened his own *yeshivah* in Worms, from where their father Rabbi Betzalel had fled many years before.

One year later, Rabbi Yaakov, the Maharal's uncle, who also lived in Worms, became chief rabbi of the entire German state. He was appointed to this post by the King of Germany himself, and so he became known as "the kaiser's rabbi."

A year later, however, persecutions of the Jews of Bavaria embittered these accomplishments.

Meanwhile, the Maharal had another daughter, Gitteleh, and after her a fourth daughter, Reichel.

The Maharal saw the importance of having children as the fulfillment of one's potential. He later wrote, "The word for son (*ben*) is from the word for building (*binyan*), for the son is the building of his father. Similarly, the word for daughter (*bas*) is grammatically derived from *banas* [and thus also related to the word *binyan*], except that [for grammatical reasons] the 'n' is not pronounced." (*Gur Aryeh*)

5

Rabbi of Nikolsburg

ALTHOUGH THE JEWISH COMMUNITY OF NIKOLSBURG WAS ONLY founded in 1450, it had already become the leading Jewish community in Moravia.

It was therefore no small honor when the young Rabbi Yehudah Loew received a formal invitation to move from Posen to Nikolsburg and fill the newly-created post of Chief Rabbi of Moravia (which also included two other well-known Jewish communities, Prossnitz and Lundenberg). This happened in 1553, when the Maharal was only thirty-nine years old.

The Maharal's early brilliance might have led others to believe that he would make a dazzling career for himself from an early age. But until this point, he seems to have contented himself with living the life of a private citizen, learning Torah and raising his family. The Maharal would live up to his early promise, but he would not be rushed to take on the burden of public leadership.

The quality of his life had been noted by other Torah sages; his name had spread, and the community of Nikolsburg invited him to begin the first phase of his public career.

"It is the glory of God to conceal a matter; it is the glory of a king to investigate a matter." (*Mishlei*) For years, the Maharal had enjoyed the privilege of serving God for the sake of Heaven, and his life had been a concealed one. Now, he knew that the time had arrived for him to become a king, a leader in the public arena.

The Maharal was quickly introduced to the quality of life in his new home.

Tall and regal, the Maharal stood at the eastern wall of the synagogue, swaying slowly, his head and body covered by a long *tallis*. The *tallis* was draped far forward, and his face could only be seen occasionally as he rocked back and forth, his eyes closed in the intense concentration of devotion. He seemed like an angel in heaven dedicating its being to the service of God.

The cantor's rich voice rolled out the syllables of the *Pesukei Dezimrah* sonorously, and the murmur of praying men accompanied him. In the balcony, some women and girls were bending over their *siddurim*, and one woman led the prayers for those who could not read.

The cantor sang forth the verses with a beauty that seemed to soar to the very heavens. If one had stood between the cantor and the Maharal, one might have felt as though the synagogue no longer stood on foreign soil but had been transported bodily to Yerushalayim itself, perhaps to the very site of the holy *Beis Hamikdash*, where the Leviim led in song and the Kohanim led in service, and all hearts soared in ecstasy to unite with their Creator.

As the cantor reached the stirring phrases of *Nishmas Kol*

THE MAHARAL

Chai—The breath of every living thing shall praise You, O God—a slight murmur that the Maharal had heard before in the recesses of his consciousness grew louder.

"If our mouths were as full of song as the sea," sang the cantor, oblivious to the murmuring, which also grew louder, precisely as the murmur of the sea itself.

"If our tongues were filled with song like the roar of its waves," the cantor sang, and indeed, the murmur also began to increase in sound like a faint yet growing roar.

"If our lips were full of praise like the spaces of the heavens," continued the cantor, and the Maharal, torn from his ecstatic prayer by the increasing clamor, turned to see what was causing the disturbance.

"Still," the cantor continued in a deep vibrato, "we could not praise You enough, O God, and bless Your Name ..." and then the vast tide of voices rose, and the remainder of the cantor's magnificent song was swiftly drowned in the great ocean of talk.

What was the cause of this extraordinary outburst? The Maharal could hear snatches of conversations on every side of him.

"... depending on the weather and the carrot crop, I think that I could see my way ..."

"... but you wouldn't believe it from the way she dresses. I hear she hires her own seamstress ..."

"... I say you're wrong, and I'm willing to wager five *thaler* on it!"

"... but since you ask, we could use some help now that my wife's father is ..."

After the *Shemoneh Esrei*, the Maharal turned to the *parnas*, the community leader, who stood at his side, and asked him, "Reb Margolis, what is all this talking?"

"What do you mean?" Reb Margolis looked at the Maharal quizzically. He drew together his eyebrows so that a vertical line appeared in his forehead, pulled in his chin and cupped his beard in his hand.

"This talking!" the Maharal said. "In the middle of the prayers. It's unheard of!"

Reb Margolis tilted his head and looked thoughtfully past the Maharal. "Perhaps it is unheard of in Posen, Rabbi Loew. But here, it cannot stop."

"Cannot stop?" the Maharal sputtered.

"Certainly not. It is the custom since I was a little boy. We are a very traditional community, and we cannot abrogate old customs."

The Maharal stared speechlessly at Reb Margolis. The *parnas*, not noticing the Maharal's amazement, blandly continued, "Oh, and my son will be *bar-mitzvah* this week. I hope you will be able to grace us with your presence."

"Oh yes," the Maharal replied, still shaken. "Of course I'll come."

The following Tuesday afternoon, the Maharal sat at the head of the banquet table next to Reb Margolis's son, who was dressed in a new, well-cut caftan, as Reb Margolis himself, his face shining, constantly jumped up to greet a new arrival or to urge the servants to do their work. The long table was set with fine cutlery. Two servants were busy filling bowls of soup and ladling meat onto plates and hurriedly bringing them to the men crowded about the table.

There was a clatter from the courtyard, and Reb Margolis again jumped up from his seat. "Ah, the wine has arrived," he announced gaily. "Karl, go take care of it."

Karl, a wall-eyed, gentile servant in bright green livery and shoes down at the heel, who had been helping bring the dishes to the table, picked up a large pitcher from a serving table and briskly stepped out.

Seeing this, the Maharal quickly got up from the table and followed the servant. In the courtyard stood a cart with a village Jew at the reins idly watching his horse's flicking tail as Karl prepared to unplug the barrel in the cart and pour wine into the jug.

"Hold it!" the Maharal called out.

Karl looked up. "I'm not doing anything wrong, sir. I'm only doing what the master told me, if you please."

"Don't be frightened," said the Maharal. "I'm not angry at you." He turned to the cart driver. "I'm surprised at you, Reb Yid," he said in Yiddish. "How can you allow a non-Jew carry your wine, when that makes it *yayin nesech*?"

The wagon driver was apparently unimpressed with the Maharal's reproof, for he continued to gaze impassively at his animal, the twitching of whose tail appeared to exercise a soporific effect upon the man's capacities.

Reb Margolis came out, rubbing his hands and attempting not to appear irritated. "Is anything the matter, Rabbi Loew? Why is the boy not bringing in the wine?"

Rabbi Loew turned sternly to Reb Margolis. "I'm surprised at you, Reb Margolis. Surely you know that by sending a non-Jew to bring the wine into your banquet, you would render the wine unkosher and cause everyone sitting at your banquet to commit a transgression."

Unexpectedly, Reb Margolis seemed relieved. "Oh, is that what you're worried about?" he said. "Please set your mind at ease. Although you are obviously a great expert in Jewish law as it is practiced in Poland, you are not yet fully conversant with the interpretation of the law here in Moravia."

"What do you mean?"

"Well, as you know," said Reb Margolis, hooking his thumbs in his belt and leaning back upon his heels, "the rabbis of the Talmud forbade wine moved by a gentile because they were afraid that an idol worshipper might dedicate it to his idol, and because they didn't want Jews to be drinking together with gentiles, which might lead to intermarriage."

THE MAHARAL

"I have come across statements to that effect, yes," observed the Maharal dryly.

"Well, as you may *not* know," Reb Margolis continued, "here in our communities, we drink wine regularly at all our meals. It would be most difficult to have to keep all the details of this law punctiliously." He loosened one hand from his belt and held it palm out, as though warding off an attack. "Which we would do most happily, I assure you, if that was what the law required." He put his hand down and replaced his thumb in his belt. "Fortunately, it doesn't." Content with this, Reb Margolis added, "And so, since the hour is late and the guests waiting, I will simply ask Karl—"

"What do you mean?" the Maharal interrupted.

Reb Margolis looked surprised and hurt. "I thought that it would be obvious to a man of your caliber. We do not consider Christians idol-worshippers, and in the normal course of things, Jews do not marry non-Jews. So there is no problem with wine that has been moved by a non-Jew."

"I am afraid that as Moravia's chief rabbi, I must ask you to defer to my *Halachic* ruling," said the Maharal, "which is to continue to prohibit such wine as unkosher."

A look of rage flashed across Reb Margolis's face, but he suddenly changed his expression and looked at the Maharal calmly. He bowed his head, tilted it to the side and clasped his hands together. "Of course," he said. "Karl," he turned to the servant. "Leave the pitcher here. Go inside and call Yentl to come out and pour the wine." He turned back to the Maharal and said smoothly, "I trust that it will suit the rabbi?"

"Thank you so much for your understanding," the Maharal replied with equal calm. "That will certainly be acceptable."

The Maharal quickly discovered that these two problems—talking in the synagogue and laxity regarding *yayin nesech*—were common in his new community. And in attempting to solve these problems, he discovered a bigger problem: the

THE MAHARAL

community seethed with conflict. His very attempts to do something about the synagogue talking and *yayin nesech* met with both fervent support and fervent opposition. It became evident early on that the battle lines between the two groups had been drawn years earlier and that they merely regarded these issues as new excuses to fight each other.

The controversies extended to many areas. Some were relatively benign—snobbery and one-up-manship, everyone attempting to appear more ostentatious than his neighbor; even this could be quite destructive, leading families to bankrupt themselves for the sake of showing off for their neighbors. Other conflicts involved those two magnets of evil: power and money. The elections of Jewish officials invited corruption and fraud. And the position of tax collector was fought over bitterly and brutally by people who sought to use the position to enrich themselves.

The Maharal's vigorous battle against this corruption resulted in the passage of a series of *takanos*, or ordinances, dealing with all these problems.

Among these ordinances were two public blessings—"*mi shebeirach*"—recited aloud in synagogues every *Shabbos* after the reading of the Torah. One of the blessings contained a warning against drinking *yayin nesech*. The other asked for Hashem's blessing for "he who guards his mouth and tongue and doesn't interrupt the prayers with even one word—not even a word of Torah—from *Baruch She'amar* and onwards, as well as during the reading of the Torah."

In the course of these battles for the rehabilitation of the Moravian communities, the Maharal was not afraid to rebuke powerful men and risk their enmity. Besides his moral strength, he had a strategic invulnerability as well. Being personally wealthy, he was not financially dependent on anyone.

The Maharal's *takanos* were a source of inspiration for many other communities as well. Some emulated them in

THE MAHARAL

modified form, and others applied to the Maharal to help formulate *takanos* for their specific situations.

The Maharal was appalled by the bickering he encountered. He regarded conflict, and particularly conflict among leaders, as the root of evil. And the Maharal saw in the making of peace the source of the existence of the world. In later years, he wrote, "When a person holds himself back during an argument, the world rests upon him. Such a person does not deviate from a balanced, middle path, and this is equivalent to causing the existence of the world." (*Nesivos Olam*)

In addition to this vital work, the Maharal also led a *yeshivah* and trained hundreds of young men to become outstanding Torah scholars and community leaders.

This was the course of work that the Maharal began when he became Chief Rabbi of Moravia in 1553, continuing for nineteen years until 1572. Although he incurred many enemies, he had many friends, people who were grateful for the presence of this tireless champion of fairness and the true intent of the Torah "whose ways are pleasantness." (*Mishlei*)

These were also turbulent times in the fields of thought and discovery. It was the exciting era of humanism and the Renaissance, when many thinkers broke free of the dogmas of the Church and freely used the results of their observation and experiments.

Some of these thinkers entertained such radical ideas that the church excommunicated and even executed them, like Giordano Bruno who was burned at the stake in 1600. Others engaged in ingenious experiments that laid the groundwork for the extraordinary network of technological sophistication that today enwraps the globe.

Copernicus (1473–1543) posited the radical idea that the sun does not orbit the earth, standing motionless at the center of the universe, but rather that the earth was but one of a number of planets revolving about the sun. Tycho Brahe

THE MAHARAL

(1546–1601) and, somewhat later, Johannes Kepler (1571–1630) produced further exacting observations of the heavens and exciting theories of how they operated. The ingenious experiments of Galilei Galileo (1564–1641) and his research in the area of astronomy and physics catapulted the world forward in discovery and invention.

In the midst of this effervescence of discovery and new concepts, many Jews became enamored of the sciences and gradually began to loosen their allegiance to the Torah.

Torah leaders responded to this burgeoning crisis in various ways. Some urged a total ban on interest in these dangerous areas. In 1559, for instance, Rabbi Aharon of Posen gave a talk in which he forbade any dealing with the new sciences, as well as with the philosophical works of the Rambam, whose rationalistic leanings, combined with the new mood, resulted in a heady and intoxicating brew.

The Maharal apparently held a different view. He himself was well-acquainted with these new arts, and his own student, Rabbi David Gans, was personally acquainted with Tycho Brahe and spent time at his observatory.

Still, the Maharal made it clear that there was an important qualitative difference between the wisdom of Torah and the insights of the secular sciences. In later years, he wrote, "What is the difference between Torah and other sciences? The other sciences do not enable a person to cling [to Hashem]. Although the sciences advance a person's intellect, this intellectual benefit does not suffice to allow him to cleave to Hashem, since Hashem is totally separated from everything else. However, a person can cling [to Hashem] through the Torah, which is His book of instruction." (*Tiferes Yisrael*)

At best, wrote the Maharal, the secular sciences are like the circumference of a wheel that, although circling the central nub, is at a distance from it.

6

The Family Circle

DURING THESE STORMY YEARS, THE MAHARAL'S FAMILY GREW LARGER. He fathered another girl, Tillah, and after her, his sixth daughter Realina and his only son Betzalel.

By this time, the Maharal's children were growing older.

One day, the Maharal called his eldest daughter Leah to speak with him in his study. The Maharal sat behind his heavy, wooden table, the wall behind him crowded with dozens of large, leather-bound volumes. Leah sat down on the chair next to the desk.

"Yes, Father?" she said. She was a tall, short-haired girl with no adornment but simple earrings. The native modesty that shone from her gave her all the ornament she needed.

"Leah, my child," the Maharal told her, "your mother and I have been talking about you."

Leah nervously smoothed the pleated folds of her dress, a

THE MAHARAL

simple outfit that hung elegantly upon her.

"Do you think you are ready to get married, child?"

Leah colored. "I—I don't know, Father. I am still young, and—"

"Of course, my dear."

After a long pause, Leah raised her head and asked hesitantly, "But may I ask, who—I mean, have you thought of anyone—?"

The Maharal laughed. "Yes, my child, I have thought of someone. Do you want to know who he is?"

Leah hung her head again modestly. "If you wish, Father."

"He is a young man named Rabbi Yitzchak Cohen, a Torah scholar with very good personal qualities, a bit of a poet, a very intelligent man who, I must tell you, Leah, is quite royal. He comes from a very fine family as well. His grandfather is Rabbi Akiva—"

"Father, do you mean Akiva the Prince?" Leah interrupted excitedly.

"Yes, I do, child," the Maharal smiled.

"Father, he is so great!"

"Yes, child," said the Maharal.

Leah had heard so much about Rabbi Akiva—Akiva the Prince, he was called. He was a fabulously wealthy man and a very learned Torah scholar. He had been an important officer in the court of King Mattiash the Pious of Uban, Hungary, until enemies had plotted against him and he had been forced to flee with his family to Prague.

There he had built a magnificent mansion and opened a *yeshivah*.

And of course, who hadn't heard of his twelve sons and thirteen daughters? He himself was a *kohein*, and he had married off twelve of his daughters to *kohanim* (the thirteenth had married a Levi). Everyone knew his saying that when he gave the *kohein's* blessing on holidays, the word *koh*—referred to him, because *koh* was numerically equivalent to twenty-five: the number of *kohanim* that included himself, his sons and sons-in-law.

"He is here in Nikolsburg," the Maharal said. "Would you like to meet him, my dear?"

"I—yes, Father."

"You are growing up. With God's help, you will soon be raising children of your own. Run along now. I am sure your mother wants to talk to you."

Leah got up slowly from the chair and walked to the door, then burst into a run, crying, "Mama, mama!" and disappeared from the room. The Maharal looked after her. She was still just a child, after all. But she was growing older.

It was not long before Leah was no longer only the Maharal's daughter but also a woman, a wife.

Soon afterwards, the Maharal's daughter Gitteleh married Rabbi Shimshon Brandeis Halevi, who later became *primus*—mayor—of Prague.

But there were not only joyous family events. In 1563, the Maharal's uncle, Rabbi Yaakov, passed away. Soon afterwards, the Maharal's brother, Rabbi Chaim, succeeded him as Chief Rabbi of Worms.

Following that, the Maharal's daughter Reichel married Rabbi Avraham Wallenstein, and she soon had a child, Moshe Segal.

And then the Maharal's daughter Tillah married Rabbi Hirsch Sabatka.

One day, a servant left Leah's house carrying a message that she was not feeling well and she would appreciate it if her sisters could visit her to cheer her.

But Leah did not improve after a few days and felt too weak to leave the house. Rabbi Yitzchak, her husband, came home to attend to her, and her father and mother also came to visit her.

THE MAHARAL

The best doctor in Nikolsburg was called. He prescribed some powders and a healing regimen, but he left shaking his head. The best doctor in the entire region was called, then the best doctors in all of Moravia.

Prayers were recited for her in all the synagogues. All those who had been helped by the Maharal, all those whose own daughters, sisters, husbands, wives and parents had been restored to life and health by the prayers of the Maharal, those whose rights had been defended by him and those who had been taught and inspired by him now prayed and recited Psalms for the health of his first-born daughter.

But the Heavenly decree was not recalled. One quiet day, Leah took leave of her family and slipped away from her husband, father, mother, sisters and brother—young, serene, childless.

Her family bewailed the loss of her brightness, her liveliness, her quick intelligence, her sense of right and wrong, her innate goodness.

One day, months after her passing away, Rabbi Yitzchak Cohen came to see the Maharal.

"Rabbi Loew," he said, "the *Chumash* tells us that 'it is not good for a man to be alone.' I would only like to marry a woman who had the same good qualities and the same good upbringing as did Leah, of blessed memory. Rabbi Loew, you have a daughter, Feigeleh, who is not yet married. Would it be presumptuous for me to speak to you of her?"

"Thank you for being so frank," said the Maharal. "We must of course ask her. But I myself am perfectly gratified. I would be glad to have you in my family again."

And a few months later, Rabbi Yitzchak married the Maharal's remaining unmarried daughter.

7

Farewell, Moravia

THE JEWS OF PRAGUE WERE OFTEN EXPELLED FROM THE CITY FOR THE crime of being Jews. But unlike such occurrences in other areas, as in the German states, they were usually allowed to return after a short period. That had occurred in 1557, and then again in 1561. At that time, Rabbi Mordechai Tzemach Katz made the long journey to Rome and pleaded before Pope Pius IV to nullify the decree.

In 1564, King Ferdinand, the author of many of these expulsions, died, and his son Maximilian II took his place. Maximilian was a liberal ruler, and to the Jews' delight, he issued a decree in 1567 revoking all previous expulsion orders.

During the rule of Maximilian II, and of his son Rudolf II after him, the Jews enjoyed what has been described as the Golden Age of Prague. In Torah learning, in intellectual

THE MAHARAL

achievement, in social progress and in economic growth, the Jews of Prague flourished. But this Golden Age of Torah study in Prague had a more immediate cause. At this time, the Maharal arrived in Prague, where he would live, off and on, for the rest of his life. And the name of the city would forever be linked with his: the Maharal of Prague.

In 1571, King Maximilian II demonstrated his amicable policy toward the Jews by visiting the ghetto of Prague together with the queen.

This splendid occasion was attended by all the Jews of Prague, headed by their greatest Torah scholars and community leaders.

Amidst the throng of Jews and government officials, the king and queen were received by the chief rabbi, surrounded by a delegation of leading Jews, dressed in their *Shabbos* finery.

The rabbi, himself royal in bearing, led the king and queen to a large, colorful canopy that fluttered in the stiff breeze.

Holding a *Sefer Torah* in his arms, the rabbi blessed the royal couple, who stood respectfully at attention and accepted his blessing in silence. Then the king spoke a few words, offering his royal greetings to the inhabitants of Prague. With that, he returned to his carriage, surrounded by brightly-dressed soldiers wearing colorful, plumed hats and armed with brilliantly shining swords. As the Jews stood at attention, the coachman flicked his whip, and the two great bay horses, their bridles festooned with plumes, shook their heads and broke into a stately trot.

The king's carriage was preceded and followed by other carriages, and as the entourage rolled out of the ghetto, the Jews looked on joyfully. The non-Jews also stared, many in puzzlement and some in dismay, at the strange sight of a monarch honoring this weak and subjugated people with his presence.

THE MAHARAL

For many days afterwards, the Jews were filled with elation. They, the downtrodden, who had been regarded as cursed and fair game for any heartless thug, had been graced with a visit of state by the new king. Their hearts soared. Might they not soon rise free from the nightmare and quagmire called history and climb to freedom and protection? Who could know, perhaps they might soon be an honored nation?

Mordechai Meisel, a leading Jew of Prague, celebrated the visit of King Maximilian by building the magnificent Klaus Synagogue on the site of the king's visit. This synagogue, which still stands today, is one of the loveliest buildings in Prague, a city known as one of the most beautiful in the world.

Mordechai Meisel, for many years head of Prague's Jewish community, was the richest Jew in Central Europe in his time. He was an advisor to the king and a great philanthropist who built a number of synagogues, a hospital and a shelter for the poor, and who paved the roads as well. At one time, he donated ten thousand *gulden* each to Posen, Cracow and Yerushalayim. (A large ox at that time cost only five *gulden*.)

A number of months after the royal visit, another occurrence took place immeasurably far from the sphere of the earth, yet filled the inhabitants of many countries with fears, hopes, foreboding and strange prophecies.

The night sky appeared normal enough. Yet in a field one evening, coming home from a weary day of studies, one sharp-eyed astronomy student called to his friend, "Look! Isn't that a new star shining there, in the north?"

"A new star!" the friend replied, and even in the dusk, it was easy to see his grin. "I'm afraid that you have been studying the bottoms of beer mugs more than your books of study."

"Yes, I suppose I must be imagining it. Yet I could have sworn that the constellation of Cassiopeia didn't contain that star."

THE MAHARAL

His friend stopped in his tracks. "You know, you're right! There's a star where no star ought to be! Listen, this is our fame! We've got to rush back to the observatory and mark our observation down!"

But they were not the only ones to note the strange phenomenon. And more mysteriously, this star kept growing in brightness until it exceeded even Venus at its brightest, until it shone even by day.

For eighteen months, this mysterious luminary shone, giving rise to speculations and predictions of the wildest sort. The crops would be spoiled! No, the crops would deliver a sevenfold harvest and the faithful would be brought upon flying ships to heaven! No, to the holy land!

Meanwhile, the plague had broken out in Moravia. The Christians turned a jaundiced eye to the Jews. The age old suspicions and slander surfaced once again. The Jews poisoned the wells! The Jews bring bad luck! The Jews prayed for this! Fear of the wrath of the surrounding gentiles and their drunken mobs was in the heart of every Jew.

And so the Jews gathered in the synagogues and prayed to God for deliverance from the flood of violence, and their leaders raced to the nobles and princes who were known to be friendly and capable of protecting the Jews if given sufficient incentive—for their good will could be purchased. But still, many Jewish lives were lost and many Jews grieved, until Maximilian II was moved to intervene in 1574 and put an end to the violence.

It was in this atmosphere that, in 1572, the Maharal presided at the general meeting of representatives of all the Jewish communities of Moravia, held in the town of Lundenberg.

Very soon afterwards, the Maharal left his post in Moravia, after having served there for nineteen years.

Why did he do so? Was it because, in the worsening

atmosphere of terror and pogrom, he felt that he could no longer serve effectively and that he would be needed elsewhere? Had he suffered any disappointments, any frustrations at the general meeting and decided that the opposition of Jews to his innovative ideas made his stay in Moravia no longer productive? Or perhaps the reason might be simply that the Maharal was now sixty years old. He had served a full and demanding career. Perhaps he thought that he should now retire and return to his private occupation of learning Torah. Unfortunately, no clue to the Maharal's reason exists.

The Maharal and his family one misty morning set out from the home where they had lived for so many years and, in a caravan of carriages, rolled out of Nikolsburg. Although there had been an official ceremony the evening before, the rabbis of the city rose early to again take leave of the Maharal and accompany him from town. Many ordinary people also walked beside the carriages, out of the town and down the bumpy road leading past broad farm fields until, one by one, they turned back home. The line of carriages continued on its way as the morning sun rose and burned away the wispy fog.

8

The Gem of Europe

PRAGUE, CITY OF A HUNDRED TOWERS; PRAGUE THE GOLDEN; AS beautiful as Florence and majestic as Rome; city of magic and the brightest gem in the crown of the world—these were the names by which Prague was known.

As the Maharal's entourage approached Prague, the road ran alongside a hill. Down the slope of the hill was a green sword of trees, and beyond that the lovely sight of a city that looked as though it had been built as a prince's toy and magically transformed to life-size. The city was a profusion of handsome, white, red-roofed buildings, many with domes and spires, and thickets of parks in their midst.

Beyond these houses was a wide and placid, gently curving river across which a series of bridges had been thrown, and on the opposite side of the river were yet more homes and magnificent public buildings, with Prague Castle dominating the skyline. The sun shone clearly and the vista seemed lightly dusted with sparkling golden particles.

Seen from here, the city was a melange of magnificent towers with their many spires, golden domes shining in the golden sun and handsome town clocks.

Soon the Maharal's carriage entered the city. Its streets bustled with magnificent Romanesque, Gothic and Renaissance architecture. The palace gardens shone in the bright sunlight, the squares were spacious, and the bridges spanning the beautiful Moldova River were crowded with stone residences and churches.

The carriage passed by narrow lanes, no more than eight feet across and with no sidewalks. White houses with gray, handsome cornices in the shape of inverted "v"s hanging above the windows rose up three and four stories to roofs of red clay tiles. Small roofed arches joined over the heads of the pedestrians, linking the houses on both sides of the street.

On the streets walked peasants in their traditional dress. The women wore white kerchiefs that surrounded their faces and were tied beneath their chins, decorated along their foreheads with blue trimming. Men and women carried vegetables, chickens, meat and bread.

The Maharal's carriage passed by houses whose doors were adorned with charming carvings that hinted at the owner's name, profession, or simply were the result of a whim: three crossed violins indicating the residence of a musician; a smiling frog; an undulating snake; a green crawfish with claws outstretched; a swan beating its silver wings; three heart-shaped strawberries painted a bright red; a tender lamb raising its front hoof; a radiating sun with a human face; a swinging ship's anchor; a mighty lion holding a lantern in one foreleg; or simply an ornate carving of a key.

The entourage soon passed this, and now they were driving through the large Old Town Square, an airy, broad

THE MAHARAL

square filled with hundreds of hawkers, squawking chickens, farmers, peasants, noblemen, squealing children, barking dogs, lowing oxen and braying donkeys.

And now, the Maharal's carriage rolled into the walled-in Jewish ghetto. The magnificent finery that the leading Jews wore as they stood at attention to welcome the Maharal could not conceal the humiliating yellow badge that each Jew had to wear upon his clothing.

The Maharal descended from the carriage and was led through the narrow streets, thronged with on-lookers, mostly Jews, but non-Jews as well, who wished to catch a glimpse of the great rabbi who had come to be the Jews' new spiritual leader.

The Maharal had a look at the Jewish ghetto's own town hall, a dull-pink building, attached to which was the high-windowed, square building called the High Synagogue.

The Maharal passed the Klaus Synagogue, which had been built just one year earlier on the site of the chief rabbi's blessing of King Maximilian. He passed more crowded, dilapidated residences, and then the Meisel Synagogue, which, like the Klaus Synagogue, had been built by Mordechai Meisel.

Now, as the Maharal walked along, he passed the Jewish cemetery. Because the authorities had not allowed Jews to expand the cemetery or to build a new one over a period of hundreds of years, it was a crowded jumble of over ten thousand tombstones, underneath which perhaps a hundred thousand Jews had been buried, in vertical layers that sometimes contained over ten bodies one above the other.

Trees and bushes grew among the thousands of headstones inscribed with Hebrew inscriptions. Many of the tombstones bore carvings of meaningful symbols. Hands giving the *kohein's* blessing symbolized a family of *kohanim*; a jug indicated a family of Leviim; a bunch of grapes was the symbol of the tribe of Yehudah; a fish marked the grave of a man named Fisch or Karpeles; the picture of a girl indicated the grave of a youngster; below a tombstone marked by a dove with an olive branch in its mouth a man named Vogel (bird) lay buried; a woman in a bodice and a long, wide dress with her hands upon her hips indicated the grave of an unmarried woman; and a woman with flowers or a wreath indicated the grave of a bride; a ram leaping with its two forefeet in the air marked the spot where a man named Lamm lay buried; a stag showed that here lay buried a man named Hirsch; a bear was marked above the grave of a man named Berl.

Next to the cemetery was the large Pinkas Synagogue, the city's oldest synagogue. And the Maharal was finally brought to the Alteneushul (Old-New Synagogue, featured on the cover of this book) the center of Prague's official Jewish life, where the chief rabbi gave his sermons on *Shabbos* and holidays.

The community leaders, led by the chief rabbi, Rabbi Yitzchak Melling, and the mayor, Mordechai Meisel, invited the Maharal proudly into the Alteneushul. The synagogue was three hundred years old, but the Jewish presence in Prague was even older. Jews in Prague had comprised the first such community in Bohemia, and one of the first in all of Europe, dating back to perhaps as early as the days of the Talmud. By the beginning of the tenth century, there were already a good number of Jews living in Prague.

The Jewish community received the Maharal with a pomp and circumstance that reflected their feeling of confidence in the era of tolerance that King Maximilian II had ushered in. Prague occupied a central place on the European map, and with the accession of King Maximilian, it was becoming the intellectual crossroads of Europe. This was good for the Jews, for the intellectual atmosphere of the time was relatively broad-minded.

The Jews were also in a favorable position from another

THE MAHARAL

point of view. The local aristocracy was responsible both for approving the king's yearly budget and for providing it. In order to come up with the ready cash, the members often turned to Jews to lend them the money—willingly or unwillingly. A number of Jews had become major money-lenders—in the absence of a more formal banking system—because they were confined to this and other undesirable professions. And because Prague had such relatively good conditions for the Jews, it became a center for Jews from all over Europe.

Even as the Maharal stood at the podium in the synagogue, he could see Jews dressed in various costumes and speaking various languages. There were Jews whose parents had been forced to leave Spain during the Inquisition; there were Italian Jews, like the Gershoni family: and there were other Jews from France, Hungary, Denmark, Poland, Turkey, and even Jews from Jerusalem. Prague was an international city in miniature. Here were Jews gathered from all over the globe, united by their shared allegiance to the Torah.

The Maharal was happy to begin this new chapter in his life after his difficult years in Nikolsburg. But his heart was heavy when he thought of his married daughters left behind. Feigeleh, for instance, was staying in Nikolsburg, for her husband Rabbi Yitzchak Katz had taken over his post to become *rosh yeshivah* and chief rabbi of Nikolsburg and Moravia.

The Maharal had not come to Prague in an official capacity. Rabbi Melling remained the Chief Rabbi. But as the Maharal shook hands with the many dignitaries and exchanged words with them, he learned that Prague suffered from much of the same dissension and conflict he had confronted in Nikolsburg.

It was not the Maharal's role to deal with this. He was a private citizen now, and his concern was primarily with private matters, including the teaching of Torah. But over the

THE MAHARAL

course of time, these matters presented themselves to the Maharal repeatedly, until he had little choice but to deal with them.

The Maharal stood one afternoon at the window of his new home, gazing out at the riot of colorful spring blossoms and thinking, What was the cause of this problem?

It seemed that there were several reasons.

First of all, because Jews had gathered here from so many cultural backgrounds, there were bound to be irritations and grievances.

Moreover, although communal power was legally shared by a group of community board members who collected taxes, appointed rabbis and judges, and represented the Jewish community to the government, the real power was in the hands of a few wealthy families. The wealthier families paid more taxes, and according to tradition, the amount of taxes one paid determined how much power one had in the community. Thus, real power was not determined by the elections but by behind-the-scenes wheeling and dealing.

Related to this, rabbis and judges were elected very frequently. This made them so dependent on the good will of the board that it was difficult for them to act courageously. And the board in turn was dependent on the concentration of power among a few families. (*Derush Al Hatorah*)

All these factors led to an atmosphere of constant tension, resentments and jockeying for power.

But at the same time, there was a spiritual ferment and intellectual freshness. The source of this nervous energy that did so much to destroy the solidarity of the community was, in essence, a positive spiritual phenomenon. In later years, the Maharal wrote, "[The Jews] are arrogant in their essential nature, because they are not physical beings. They are like fire, which is very active, because it acts with great strength." (*Nesivos Olam*) It was the misplaced spiritual energy of the

THE MAHARAL

Jews that was causing so much irritation.

The Maharal gazed at the profusion of white and pink blossoms on the trees that spread out beyond Prague. Trees grew fruit naturally, but they needed the active grafting and pruning of man to produce good and sweet fruit. So it was with the Jews. It was not enough that they express their innermost being naturally. There must be a gardener, a leader who would guide them so that they would express their souls' energy in the most refined manner.

The Maharal turned from the window. It was not yet time for him to become a private citizen.

9

A Lesson in Learning

RABBI MELLING, CHIEF RABBI OF PRAGUE, WAS A NOTED TORAH scholar. In his *yeshivah*, many students toiled over the Talmud, and outside of the four cubits of study, he was known as a good and charitable man.

But the Maharal was a giant, a pillar of his age. It was no slight to Rabbi Melling that the Jews of Prague began to gravitate to the Maharal's magnetic personality.

Mordechai Meisel, mayor of the Jews, came to the Maharal one morning. Meisel was dressed superbly, wearing a loose-fitting cloak with a collar that circled his neck as high as his ear, and then cut sharply down so as not to interfere with his elegant beard. On his head, he wore a chaperon, a soft cloth hat that rather resembled a turban. The cloak did not have sleeves, but his arms extended from long slits in the material. The cloak ended at his knees, where high, tight stockings descended from knee-length breeches to leather shoes without laces.

"What may I do for you, Rabbi Loew?" Meisel asked, bowing slightly and spreading out his arm. "I am completely at your service."

"I am grateful for your offer," the Maharal replied. "There is one thing I would like to see, and that is to see how people learn Torah here in Prague."

"I don't understand, Rabbi Loew," replied Meisel. "We learn Talmud, *Halachah*, the *meforshim*—what other way to learn is there?"

"Let us go visit the *yeshivos*, and perhaps my meaning will become clearer."

The two men set out into the cool morning and walked down the lane to a *yeshivah* from which they heard the voice of a rabbi giving a *shiur*—a lecture—on a chapter of the Talmud. The Maharal and Meisel entered the study hall unobtrusively and stood at the back. Before them, about twenty students in their late teens and early twenties were sitting at a table, volumes of the Talmud before them, while a white-haired rabbi wearing a floppy cloth hat sat at their head, speaking vigorously and waving his thumb through the air. When he saw the Maharal and Meisel enter the room, he interrupted himself in mid-sentence and rose to his feet, and the students, turning their faces about, also stood up.

The Maharal motioned them to sit down. "Please go on with your lesson," he said. "Do not pay any attention to us."

The rabbi and his students sat, and the rabbi continued the thread of his argument.

The Maharal and Meisel listened to his *shiur* for a few minutes. By interpreting the text of an unclear *Tosafos* in a rather peculiar manner, the rabbi showed that the *Tosafos* was possibly disagreeing with the commentary of the Ran on an entirely different Talmud section. However, by bringing in

THE MAHARAL

a comment of the Rif on yet a third, unrelated section of the Talmud, he attempted to demonstrate that one could actually suggest a way to reconcile everything—assuming that one relied on a subtly implied principle that one could infer from a *halachah* brought by the Rambam in yet another, unrelated area. Thus, when one returned to the *Tosafos*, one could read it in a manner that resolved the original, apparent disagreement with the Ran—at the price, however, of having to understand the *Tosafos* to be actually saying almost the opposite of what it appeared to be saying. But at any rate, the lecture had nothing to do with the actual topic of the Talmud, nor had it anything to do with learning how to derive actual *halachah* from the laws discussed there.

After fifteen minutes, the Maharal slipped out the door, followed by Mordechai Meisel. When they reached the street, the Maharal said to Meisel, "Now tell me, what did you think of the style of that *shiur*?"

"I am sorry, Rabbi Loew, but I still don't understand what you mean," Meisel replied. "How can a *shiur* have a style? The Talmud is the Talmud, and the great commentators are the great commentators. A *shiur* teaches what the commentators have to say about the Talmud."

"It is not so simple, Reb Mordechai," the Maharal replied. "A *shiur* can be many things. It can have the purpose of clarifying the Talmud and teaching it in such a way so that the student himself learns how to derive the *halachah*. Or it can be used as the basis of intellectual gymnastics that do nothing to clarify the Talmud but rather confuse the students' understanding. A *shiur* can be used to illuminate the path of truth, or it can be used to confound students in a thicket of confusion."

"And the *shiur* we just heard. . .?"

"What do you think, Reb Meisel?" asked the Maharal. "Do you feel you understand more now that you heard it?"

THE MAHARAL

"No," said Meisel. "In fact, I feel quite stupid, as though the real meaning of the Talmud is something so complex and unclear that I could never understand anything. I feel disheartened. And that is odd, because if you don't mind my boasting, I am not a stupid man. I have, with God's help, accomplished a great deal. I deal with the greatest merchants of Europe and with the highest government officials in Prague. Yet when I listen to such a Talmud *shiur*, I feel hopelessly inadequate."

The Maharal sighed. "That is exactly what I am talking about, Reb Meisel," he said. "No Jew of any intelligence should feel that the Torah is something that makes him feel there is something wrong with him. When Torah is studied correctly, it is clear and makes a person happy. 'The Torah of God is perfect, it restores the soul...the *mitzvah* of God is clear, it illumines the eyes.' (*Tehillim* 19) There is a style of *shiur* that teaches the Torah in a way of darkness; and there is a style of *shiur* that teaches the Torah in a way of light."

Mordechai Meisel nodded excitedly. "What you are saying making a great deal of sense," he said. And then he mused, more to himself than to the Maharal, "To learn the Torah simply, for the sake of clarity...where can one find that?"

"Let us go on," the Maharal replied. "I would like to see a class of younger students learning Torah."

They walked another few minutes down narrow, twisting lanes and entered a square. From a number of first-floor windows whose shutters were opened to admit the light, they heard the voices of young students. Again, the Maharal and Mordechai Meisel entered and after the initial hubbub asked the class to continue learning. Besides the rabbi, there was another adult in the class, the father of a twelve-year-old boy, who had come to see how well his son was learning.

The rabbi called on the son to recite. The boy leaned over a heavy volume of the Talmud and began to read the words and translate them. Soon after that, he read the *Rashi* and translated it, and he then read a *Tosafos* and translated that. Following that, he entered into a complicated and difficult discussion of the *Tosafos*.

"Listen to his voice," the Maharal whispered to Meisel. The boy was speaking mechanically, as though he were reciting from memory.

"He doesn't seem to understand what he is saying," Meisel whispered back.

"We will see."

The boy's recitation came to an end. The rabbi praised him, and the proud father beamed down at him.

The Maharal called out, "May I ask the boy to come here so that I may ask him a few questions?"

The boy looked up with fearful eyes, but the rabbi and his father said together, "Of course, Rabbi Loew!"

"Boys, go over the page, and try to learn it as beautifully as Binyamin just did," said the *rebbe*.

Binyamin, flanked by his father and his *rebbe*, came to the end of the room and stood before the Maharal.

The Maharal looked down at the boy. "Now don't be frightened, Binyamin," he said. "I just want to ask you a few questions."

Binyamin swallowed and nodded his head.

The Maharal asked a basic question on the discussion of the *Tosafos* the boy had earlier recited. The boy began to repeat what he had said word for word, but the Maharal interrupted him and asked him a question that would make it necessary for him to think about what he was saying and answer in his own words.

The boy began to stammer, unable to reply.

"That's quite all right," the Maharal soothed him.

The Maharal then asked a question on the simple meaning of the *Tosafos*. But the boy was confused about this as well, and his answer barely made any sense.

THE MAHARAL

The Maharal asked the boy about the meaning of the Talmud with *Rashi*, but even here, it turned out, the boy didn't have a clear grasp of the text.

Finally, the Maharal asked the boy to read and translate the *Mishnah* that the Talmud text was based on. The boy stumbled over the words.

The Maharal turned to the teacher and said, "You are teaching the boy complex arguments about the *Tosafos* when he cannot even understand the basic text of the *Mishnah*. Wouldn't it be wiser to teach the students step by step? In fact, might it not be a better idea if a student of such a young age did not learn the Talmud at all, but concentrated a few years on just learning *Mishnah* clearly? As *Pirkei Avos* states, 'Five years old for *Mikrah* (*Chumash*), ten years old for *Mishnah*, thirteen years old for [learning the laws of] *mitzvos*, fifteen for learning *Gemara* [Talmud].'" (*Gur Aryeh*)

But the father interrupted before the teacher had a chance to reply. "With all due respect, Rabbi Loew, I want my son to be a Torah scholar. This is the way all children learn. If I were to teach him only *Mishnah*, the boy would be a laughingstock."

The Maharal nodded. "I am afraid you are right." He put his hand on the boy's head. "May God bring you success in your learning." He motioned to Meisel, and they left the classroom.

Outside in the street, the Maharal said to Meisel, "I firmly believe that a young student should spend several years learning only *Mishnah* before he even looks at the Talmud. Then his Talmud learning will be a hundred times easier for him. (*Gur Aryeh*) But the teachers and the parents don't want to do this, because they are so afraid that their boy might appear to be backward and never have a chance to become a Torah scholar. (*Nesivos Olam*) Besides this, I don't see why teachers are so eager to teach *Tosafos*—except that the printer happened to have put it on the same page as the Talmud text.

THE MAHARAL

(*Gur Aryeh*) I myself prefer to concentrate on the Rosh." (*Nesivos Olam*)

"According to what you are saying," Meisel replied, "a young person would really have a much better chance of becoming a Torah scholar if he put off his Talmud learning for a few years."

The Maharal nodded. "Now I would like to see how children learn in a *cheder*," he said. "May we do that?"

"Certainly, Rabbi Loew."

They retraced their steps across the square, entered another winding lane and came to a building outside of which a handful of eight-, nine- and ten-year-old boys were running about. When the boys' teacher noticed the Maharal and Mordechai Meisel, he hurried over to them and exclaimed, "It is an honor to have such distinguished visitors!"

"It is our privilege to visit a teacher of Torah," the Maharal replied. "We would like to test one of your young students."

"Certainly!" The teacher turned away. "Berel, come here a moment."

A nine-year-old child ran up to the teacher, and together they returned to the Maharal and Meisel. This was a smiling, bright-eyed child who looked up curiously at the tall figure of the Maharal.

"Berel, could you please tell me what you have been learning?" asked the Maharal.

Berel immediately began swaying back and forth, reciting the opening verses of the week's Torah reading and translating them. After each verse, he recited *Rashi* by memory and translated that as well.

The Maharal interrupted the boy's eager recitation. "Could you please explain the last *Rashi* in your own words?"

The boy was bewildered and looked up at his teacher for help.

"Tell Rabbi Loew what the *Rashi* means," the teacher

THE MAHARAL

urged the boy. But the boy was unable to.

"That's all right," said the Maharal. "Berel, could you translate this verse for me?" And he recited a verse that came from the middle of the previous week's Torah reading.

All the boy's enthusiasm was gone. He shook his head, looking down at the ground. The Maharal tousled the boy's hair and said, "Very good, Berel. You can go back to play."

The teacher quickly explained, "The boys only have time to learn the first few verses of each week's Torah reading. They never get as far as the middle of the reading."

"So when do they get to learn the entire *Chumash*?"

The teacher answered vaguely, "Oh, you know, after they grow older, on their own time..."

"Thank you very much," the Maharal told the teacher, dismissing him. He turned to Meisel and said to him, "Do you see? Children are taught difficult *Rashi* before they are able to understand them, as though a comment of *Rashi* is just something to memorize. (*Gur Aryeh*) And students are never given a foundation in learning the *Chumash*, so that they end up not knowing it at all. (*Gur Aryeh*) They are expected to somehow learn it in their spare time when they are older and already learning Talmud—after skipping the *Mishnah*, of course."

"But that's the way Jews have always learned Torah," Meisel protested.

"Is it?" the Maharal said. "Remember the *Mishnah*: 'Five years old for *Mikrah* (*Chumash*), ten years old for *Mishnah*, thirteen years old for [learning the laws of] *mitzvos*, fifteen for learning *Gemara*.'"

They began walking back in the direction from which they had set out.

"Do not think I consider myself so superior," said the Maharal. "When I started learning, I also followed this approach. But I soon realized how much I was missing. Yes, I

THE MAHARAL

have a lot of lost time to grieve for." (*Derech Hachaim*)

The Maharal sighed. "People are so foolish", he continued. They force a child to learn Talmud with *Tosafos*, and when they see his mind improving, they attribute it to the learning. Blindness! They don't realize that the child's mind was naturally maturing on its own, and the *Tosafos* had nothing to do with it. (*Gur Aryeh*) What a waste! When a youngster, aged eight or nine, learns Talmud, it is totally beyond his abilities, and such learning cannot last. (*Tiferes Yisrael*)

"In fact," the Maharal went on, "the present system of learning is so faulty that if you kept a youngster out of school and he began to learn only later on, he would in a very short time catch up to a person who had struggled for years through the system. (*Gur Aryeh*)

"But even worse, after being made to learn material beyond their capabilities, students are forced to learn false *pilpul*. Indeed," the Maharal said firmly, "it would be better for them to learn a craft such as carpentry. Carpentry, at least, like true Torah, aims at a true effect. But the purpose of false *pilpul* is falsehood. (*Tiferes Yisrael*)

"So what do I propose? I propose that students cover a great amount of material. There is no doubt that if they did this, they would know many tractates before they were married. (*Gur Aryeh*) Of course, they should also be regularly reviewing what they learn. They should learn in order: *Chumash*, *Mishnah*, and then the basic meaning of the Talmud—until they really understand what they are learning. But now, they have nothing. And why? Because they are all concentrating on things beyond the essential basics, such as *Tosafos*—which are truly extra [a *hosafah*]." (*Gur Aryeh*) He stopped and looked at Mordechai Meisel. "Now tell me, wouldn't it have been better if they had first learned the text of the Talmud itself? (*Gur Aryeh*)

"I would like to open a *beis midrash* where students can

THE MAHARAL

learn in a clear way, in a manner that seeks the true intent of what the Torah wishes to teach us."

"You are right, absolutely right!" Meisel said enthusiastically. "Though you do not need my agreement of course. And I think I understand why you brought me along today. But there was no need. Whatever you desire, I will be happy to do for you. If you wish, I will supply the Klaus Synagogue for the site of the *beis midrash*."

They passed under a tree that had showered the ground with pink and white blossom petals. The Maharal made a blessing and breathed the intoxicating scent. "What an aroma, Reb Meisel! But true Torah learning is much sweeter. With God's help, you and I shall begin a new path in learning Torah—a new path that is really an old path."

The Maharal's *beis midrash* in the Klaus Synagogue soon became a thriving center of Torah learning. The Maharal's student, Rabbi David Gans, later referred to it as a *beis vaad lachachamim*—a meeting place for the wise.

The Maharal's *beis midrash* stressed learning with a clear approach to the texts. The Maharal demanded that his students engage in constant review, so that the material would become second nature to them. In addition, he required that his students learn in groups, so that they would gain from the intellectual ferment brought about by their interplay.

Also, the Maharal frowned upon the isolated learning of *halachic* manuals, such as the *Shulchan Aruch*. He preferred that students know how to trace *halachos* back to the Talmud itself.

In addition to this, the Maharal instituted *Chevros Mishnayos*, groups of adults who would concentrate on learning *Mishnah*, as the foundation to a clear understanding of the Talmud. The Maharal's intent was not that people should skim through the *Mishnah*, but that they should understand it thoroughly. In this, too, the Maharal stressed the importance of constant review.

Old study habits were deeply entrenched, and the Maharal encountered much opposition from those who feared that he was upsetting the accepted way of doing things. But slowly, the Maharal's approach began to have an influence. In particular, the institution of the *Chevros Mishnayos* began to gain in popularity and eventually spread past Prague to many Jewish communities across Europe.

Rabbi Yom Tov Lippman Heller, a disciple of the Maharal, was inspired to write a commentary on the *Mishnah* called *Tosafos Yom Tov*, which is printed in most editions of the *Mishnah* to this very day. The establishment of the *Chevros Mishnayos* and the availability of comprehensive interpretations made the study of the *Mishnah* stronger in all Jewish communities, thanks to the Maharal's initiative.

10

King Rudolph II

THE MAHARAL'S FAMILY WAS GROWING. THE MAHARAL'S DAUGHTER, Realina, married Rabbi Chaim, who was to become the mayor of Jewish Prague for forty years.

Rabbi Chaim, a wealthy and pious man, established a number of *chadarim* and *yeshivos*, as well as a fund to support the poor.

Realina herself was a successful businesswoman, and she too acted charitably, supporting indigent Torah scholars. In addition, the Maharal's daughter Tillah had a son, Meir Sabatka. And then his daughter Feigeleh had a son, Chaim. Then Feigeleh had a second son, Naftali Katz.

And the Maharal's only son Betzalel was married and soon had his first child, whom he named Shmuel.

One morning in the year of 1576, the citizens of Prague were awakened by the mournful tolling of bells from the city's many bell towers. After serving as the king of Bohemia for twelve years, Maximilian II had died. His son Rudolf II took his place.

One of Rudolf's first moves was to begin to shift the seat of his government from Vienna to Prague, a move that was fully completed by 1583. This move was good for the Jews. From then on, the Jews of Prague, the central Jewish community in Bohemia, would have access to the highest officials of the Bohemian government.

Rudolf II was a humanist, and his devotion to literature, the arts and science made him one of the greatest cultural patrons of his day; in his surroundings, these flourished and blossomed. The scientists and thinkers of Rudolf II's time were interested not only in material phenomena but also with spiritual or magical processes. Thus, there was a great interest in alchemy, a spiritual art whose practical side promised the transformation of base metals, such as lead, into precious silver and gold.

Rudolf himself was a firm believer in these arts, and his court was filled with all types of alchemists, astrologers, other such magical and mystical explorers and an odd bunch of hucksters and self-serving purveyors of mysterious skills.

Over the course of the century, many non-Jews had focused their mystical interest on the newly-published works of Kabbalah and had developed a school of so-called Christian Kabbalah. These men twisted Kabbalah to make it conform to Christian theology. At one point, works of Kabbalah were even ordered translated into Latin by the Pope, so that Christian divinity students could make use of them.

Not surprisingly, an interest in Kabbalah was an integral part of life at Rudolf II's court. Besides this, Rudolf II had direct contact with the Jews themselves, such as Mordechai Meisel, who dealt regularly with the court. And in addition, a number of Rudolf's closest servants were apostate Jews.

THE MAHARAL

With all this, it is no wonder that the king should eventually hear of a great Jewish leader living in Prague who was reputed to be a master Kabbalist. It is also no wonder that the king, who encouraged every sort of person who claimed some kind of mystical or magical talent, should at some point develop an interest in meeting the Maharal.

And eventually, the king actually did meet with the Maharal. But that did not come about for many years.

But those who sew upon the tapestry of Jewish history with needles of imagination, using the brilliant threads of legend, have left many stories about clandestine and mysterious meetings between the king and the Maharal, at which the Maharal displayed the fabulous powers he had gained in his many years as a pious, holy man. Let us look in on one of these supposed meetings.

The king leaned forward, resting his hands upon the arms of his throne, listening to the standing figure who spoke in a measured and solemn tone.

"You have asked me to show you the Patriarchs and the twelve sons of Yaakov," the Maharal was saying to the king. "I have told you that I do not consider your request well-considered."

"And I have told you that it is necessary to my alchemical investigations."

"Yes, your majesty, so you have informed me. Yet you are requesting that I deal with spiritual forces that are more powerful than one is used to dealing with in alchemical investigations."

"Still—"

"Still, since your majesty has requested it of me, I shall do your bidding."

The king relaxed. His sharp eagerness softened, and he leaned back, smiling.

"But there is one condition I must make."

THE MAHARAL

King Rudolf again leaned forward, the smile gone from his face. "Yes?"

"When you see the vision that you have requested, neither you nor anyone else present may laugh."

"Laugh? Why should anyone desire to laugh?"

"Nevertheless, that must be clearly understood."

"Certainly. I shall make that very clear to all my alchemists who will be attending your...demonstration."

The date and time were set for the forthcoming supernatural manifestation.

The next evening, King Rudolf led a procession of twenty alchemists, magicians and mystics from the main meeting room of his immense palace through long halls lined with ornately-framed portraits, hanging tapestries, through large rooms whose ceilings were a fresco of romping figures, and then, as they continued, down narrow staircases and through narrow corridors that led to an isolated and secluded section of the palace.

Rudolf and a number of his guests now lit the torches they had been carrying and walked through gloomy, deserted corridors until they came to a sturdy, oak door.

"But where is the rabbi?" one of the magicians asked King Rudolf.

King Rudolf shook his head in annoyance. "I did not ask him how he is getting here, and he did not inform me."

King Rudolf put a large, embellished key into the keyhole and unlocked the door. He had to push against the door with all his might before it opened with a tearing groan.

King Rudolf and the twenty men stepped gingerly into the large, empty room. There was a high window in the far corner of the room, but night had already fallen and it was black. They looked around, but the Maharal wasn't there. A few men murmured but the king growled at them, "Silence!" and they subsided.

THE MAHARAL

The flickering torches cast crazy shadows on the ceiling and walls. How long would they have to wait here? Where was the Maharal? Would he really show up? And how would he manage to do so? For long minutes, the men stood in silence as grotesque shadows flickered.

"Good evening, gentlemen."

The men started and turned to the direction of the deep, calm voice. There, standing by the tall window, stood the Maharal.

"How did you get here?"

"That corner was empty a moment ago."

"Please, gentleman," the Maharal's voice rose over the hubbub. "You have come here for a purpose. Let us not be distracted by circumstantial matters. King Rudolf, have you told each of these present the condition of this presentation?"

"You may rely on me," the king replied. "These men have been warned that no one is to laugh no matter what cause may impel him to do so."

"I am glad," replied the Maharal. "Then I think it is time to begin."

The Maharal gave a sudden movement and to the group's immense surprise, his figure no longer stood at the window. Instead, the window was illumined, as though it looked out on a sunny desert oasis.

A little distance from a copse of palm trees stood a large tent, outside of which a few camels were tethered. In the distance, a large herd of sheep was grazing on some sparse vegetation. The tent had been pitched directly at a crossroads. Even as the men watched, a pair of riders on camels appeared out of the desert and rode up to the tent, their backs to the men in the room.

A man came out of the tent to greet them, a tall, white-haired figure in a long tunic with tassels at its corners, and with a short, white cloak tossed about his neck. As the man approached his two guests and appeared to come closer to the window, the men in the room shrank back. The man's face seemed to be a shining mirror blazing with great holiness and love.

"This is Avraham," came the voice of the Maharal.

The scene faded away. Then the window again was illuminated. Now there appeared a field, a long, grassy valley between two gently undulating hills. Onto the field walked a bearded figure. He raised his arms, closed his eyes and turned his face upward as his lips moved in prayer. He seemed to grow closer to the window. His face, suffused with holy passion, overpowered the men with fear, for in the midst of its ecstasy, there was an immense sense of awe, a terrible severity.

Now this image began to fade out, and the Maharal's calm voice announced, "That was Yitzchak."

Next they saw a scene of the dawn, lit by the rays of the rising sun. They were looking at the top of a mountain, where a man was lying with his back to them, his head resting on what appeared to be a heap of stones. But even as they watched, the stones melted together and formed one oblong, solid rock. The man awoke from his sleep. His back to the window, he poured water over his hands from a pitcher that stood at his side and stood up. He bent over, picked up the rock that had served as his pillow and stood it up as a pillar. As he turned to pick up a jar of oil, the men in the room caught a glimpse of his face. His features were a perfect blend of the great lovingkindness they had seen in Avraham and the awesome strictness they had seen in Yitzchok, and the combination gave him an overpowering beauty of holiness. Then the image started to fade away.

"That was Yaakov," said the voice of the Maharal.

Now, in quicker succession, the twelve sons of Yaakov began to pass before the awed men.

THE MAHARAL

First they saw Reuven, a young man gathering the fragrant mandrake plants from among the stalks of grain.

Then they saw Shimon, a mighty soldier, standing among the frightened officers of Pharaoh.

After him came Levi, his sword in hand, making his way through the deserted streets of Shechem.

Then there was Yehudah, dressed in regal clothing, before whom King Rudolf felt impelled to bow his knee.

Yehudah faded out, and Zevulun took his place, a sailor guiding his ship through tempestuous waves that rose on both sides of him.

Then they saw Yissachar, sitting at the entrance of a tent and learning, as outside in the fields, the grains and crops grew plentifully, succulent and swollen.

Dan appeared next, dressed in armor, and after him, Gad, leading a mighty force of troops.

After these two military leaders, they saw Asher, carrying savory dishes of meat, pastry and fresh fruit, so sweet they could smell their intoxicating aroma.

This too faded away, and now they saw Naftali, "a deer running free." Naftali, his bright red hair streaming backwards, his face covered with freckles, was racing across the fields at breakneck speed to reach his brothers, his legs and arms pumping hard.

What a funny scene! Rudolph burst into a loud guffaw—then, shocked at himself, subsided into sudden silence.

But it was too late. The mystic screen of the window went black, and the room was again lit only by the light of the wildly flickering torches.

"Look!" cried one of the men, his shaking hand pointing upwards. The mass of disconcerted men gazed up. The high ceiling of the chamber was descending upon them, ready to inexorably crush them.

The panic-stricken men tried to dash to the door, but their

legs were stuck to the floor. They broke into wails of terror. Some began praying. Others called for help. Others looked up in abject terror, screaming and moaning unintelligibly.

"Rabbi Loew!" boomed out the voice of King Rudolf. "Rabbi Loew, save us!"

Again, the figure of the Maharal appeared in the corner of the room. Raising his hands into the air, his cape flowing down from his arms, the Maharal whispered secret words of Kabbalistic intent, filling them with cryptic mental significance, and the ceiling, which had come down directly over the heads of the panic-stricken men, halted, and the straining men could move their legs again.

"Forgive me, Rabbi Loew," proclaimed King Rudolf. "You were right. There are forces of holiness that are greater than my abilities. I should not have prevailed upon you. This room shall be forever sealed, and as long as this castle continues to stand, this room shall be a secret testimonial to the great mastery of your powers."

11

First Fruits

THE MAHARAL HAD REASON AGAIN TO REJOICE. HIS DAUGHTER Feigeleh gave birth to a baby girl, Chavah.

Then, in 1577, the Maharal's brother, Rabbi Chaim, was confined to his house for two months during a dreadful plague. During that time, he wrote *Sefer Hachaim* on ethics and explanations of *Chumash*, a work that, in a later generation, Rabbi Yehoshua Heschel of Apta said was written with divine inspiration.

A year later, the Maharal himself wrote a *sefer*. He was already sixty-six years old. The *sefer* was his first and he named it *Gur Aryeh*.

This work was a discussion of Rashi's commentary on the *Chumash*. In this, the Maharal was working in a form prevalent at that time. His brother's *Be'er Chaim*; Rabbi Elenburg's *Minchas Yehudah*; *Levush Ha'orah* of Rabbi Mordechai

Yaffe; *Divrei David* of the Taz; these too were commentaries on Rashi.

Often in *Gur Aryeh*, the commentary was merely a jumping-off spot for the Maharal to present his views and approaches in other areas. Here, he first explicated his approach to *Aggadah*.

In the Maharal's day, a breach had formed between those who wished to learn Torah rationally and those who wished to emphasize the mystical aspects. Only a few decades earlier, the Rambam's *Moreh Nevuchim (The Guide to the Perplexed)* had been published. This work, the Maharal was to write in a later *sefer*, "was meant for the Rambam's generation, when people were drawn after the views of the gentile philosophers, upon whom the light of Torah had not shone. If the Rambam had not written *Moreh Nevuchim*, the Jews of his time might have ceased to give any credence whatsoever to the words of the *Chumash*. That is why he interpreted the *Chumash* in a way they could understand." (*Derech Hachaim*)

But now, people were being drawn after this rationalistic spirit in ways contrary to the Torah. In particular, Jews began to view the Talmud as a document whose statements should be understood only on their surface level. As a result, many Jews, confronted by such things as seemingly-unbelievable *Aggados*, began to show disrespect to the words of the Talmud.

On the other hand, a spirit of mysticism was spreading among the Jews. Only a few years after the publication of *Moreh Nevuchim*, the *Zohar* had been published.

Most Jews treated each word of the Torah, including the *Aggados* of the Talmud, with great awe and respect. Many of them believed that these *Aggados* must all be understood literally.

The Maharal stated his view that the *Aggados* contained great meaning and mystical secrets. But this did not mean that

THE MAHARAL

each *Aggadah* must be understood according to its literal meaning. For instance, the *Midrash* said that Vashti, queen of Achashveirosh, grew a tail. This, said the Maharal, was a symbolic way of stating that she was acting in an animalistic fashion.

In *Gur Aryeh*, the Maharal also gave many examples of his clear approach to deriving the *halachah* from the Talmud without recourse to *chidudim* or *pilpul*.

This was a very controversial point. The great Rabbi Yaakov Pollack, the developer of the method of *chidudim*, had taught in Prague. In stating his opinion, therefore, the Maharal risked drawing upon his head the wrath of the admirers of Rabbi Pollack.

In addition, he criticized *darshanim*—preachers—for having recourse to false interpretations of verses merely to make a point.

Most of all, the Maharal spoke out forcefully against the corruption that threatened the communal leadership of Prague.

In his writings, as in his communal activities, the Maharal displayed great courage. He was not afraid to speak his mind forcefully and candidly. Confident that he spoke for the sake of truth and the good of the Jewish community, the Maharal did not allow any considerations of personal well-being censor his forthright comments. What might occur to him as a result of his stating the truth as he understood it was not his business; what did concern him was that he not stifle his impulse for the good, just as the prophet had no right to suppress a message from Heaven.

12

Advocate of Peace

A PUFF OF SMOKE, A RIDER'S CRY, AND UPON WHICH SAT A THIN figure leaning forward in the headlong down the road leading out of Prague, coming in and out of view from behind the trees that bordered the winding road.

Swiftly, the horse plunged on. "Rabbi Loew! Rabbi Loew!" called the hasty rider, and his shout echoed through the quiet woods.

The Maharal stepped onto the quiet road from the peaceful, leafy columns of trees, where only the chirping of birds broke the silence of the clear air. He had gone there to meditate upon his philosophy, at the point where emotion blended with intellect and rose in the flame of spirit.

The speeding rider came galloping and, seeing the Maharal standing solemnly at the side of the road, reined in his horse and leaped to the ground.

THE MAHARAL

It was Mordechai Tzemach Kohein, one of the community's most noted and wealthy patrons.

"Rabbi Loew, a thousand apologies for disturbing you!" Even as Tzemach began to speak, a carriage with two horses left the city at breakneck speed. "King Rudolf has just threatened to dissolve the delegation of five rabbis, and he demands an immediate response from the community. I rushed here to find you. A carriage is following to bring you back to the town hall, where an emergency meeting has just gone into session."

The Maharal heard the news in grave silence. A few minutes later, the carriage rolled to a halt before the two men. When the Maharal entered the carriage, the coachman maneuvered the horses around and, snapping his long whip over their heads, headed back up the hill to the city.

"I'll see you at the town meeting," Mordechai Tzemach called out. He swung onto his horse and rode up ahead of the carriage, until he rounded a corner and was lost to sight.

By the time the Maharal got out of the carriage and entered the town hall, the meeting was already in progress, and Jacob Bassevi von Treuenberg, another important community leader, was speaking.

"A shame and a disgrace! I will just take a minute to review the record, gentlemen, I believe that it is important that we recall the context and history of this unhappy affair.

"As you know, the custom in Prague has been for the community to elect twenty leading citizens to act as its community board, one of whom serves as mayor.

"And as you also know, these twenty posts have been so coveted by men who sought their own aggrandizement rather than the good of the community—"

Shouts rang out.

"Chairman, I protest!"

"You aren't letting the community heal!"

"*Lashon hara!*"

THE MAHARAL

"Quiet!" Mordechai Meisel banged his hand on the table. "Everyone will have his say. No interruptions will be allowed."

"Thank you, Reb. Meisel. As I was saying, these posts have been so coveted that men have schemed, connived, plotted, cheated, stabbed in the back, pilloried, abused and acted so disreputably that Prague has become a byword—"

"I protest again, chairman!"

"I shall not be deterred—a byword in all the Jewish communities for controversy and contention, and we have become the laughing-stock of the gentiles who look at us, and say, Is this the people who claim that they are chosen?"

"Please get to the point," Mordechai Meisel interrupted.

"I am doing so. So disgraceful did the situation become that the king himself intervened and appointed a council of five rabbis from Germany to oversee the elections and rearrange the election laws to put an end to the fraud and corruption that have so afflicted our community.

"But now King Rudolf, so sickened by the display of bickering and squabbling, and it is a sickening sight, I assure you, gentlemen, has said that he will send the council of these five rabbis home and return us to our previous situation.

"Some members here declare that we should acquiesce to the king's desire, that it is an insult to our community that we be ruled by rabbis from another state, and that we can rule ourselves.

"But I will not mince words, gentlemen, those who speak this way are either duped or attempting to dupe—"

"How long must we sit here and listen—"

"Silence, you have gone too far!"

Again, Treuenberg raised his voice over the protests. "No, I will *not* be silent, and I *will* go on, until the end of the time allotted me. Only these people can be in favor of such a move. All others, all who are mature, intelligent and recall the evil we suffered before this council began its work know that the council must be allowed to remain here and continue its work until all the corruption is uprooted. The Jews of Prague must again raise their heads in pride that we have laws that do not allow self-interested parties to manipulate and conspire to pervert the commonwealth in order to serve their petty interests."

"Your time is up," declared Mordechai Meisel. "And now we will have the great honor to invite Rabbi Loew to speak, if he so chooses."

The Maharal cleared his throat. The company of men stood a moment in respect. One wizened man, looking at the Maharal with a sour expression, only rose up half-way from his seat before sitting down again, and those about him watched him carefully and followed his example. This group had profited greatly from the corruption of earlier years, and deeply resented all impetus for change.

"What Mr. Treuenberg has stated is entirely correct," said the Maharal. "It is imperative that the council of five rabbis remain and continue its vital work. I urge each and every one of you to support the council, so that our delegation can come to King Rudolf and tell him that the Jews of Prague are solidly united on this issue.

"Due to the vital nature of this matter, every synagogue in Prague should make a special prayer this coming *Shabbos*, a *mi shebeirach* whose text I will compose, for the success of the delegation to King Rudolf."

"Does anyone else have anything to say?" asked Mordechai Meisel.

The wizened man and his cronies exchanged glances, and the man shook his head. He would not risk a head-to-head fight with the Maharal.

"In that case, the delegation shall be sent out immediately with the authorization to inform the king that the community of Prague unanimously supports the continuation of the council of five rabbis. All in favor, say aye."

The entire room resounded with ayes.

"All opposed?"

There was silence.

"The motion is therefore passed. Meeting adjourned."

The delegation was swiftly sent to Rudolf and that *Shabbos*, awaiting the decision of the king, a *mi shebeirach* for its success was recited in all the synagogues in Prague.

The Maharal prayed for the success of the Jews' request. But he knew that even if he succeeded in this, the battle was far from over. Too much that was not healthy, too much that was in imitation of the customs and corruptions of the gentile governments among which they lived, had seeped into Jewish life.

On Sunday, the Maharal mused on these matters as he took a stroll in the fertile forest outside the city. The air smelled freshly of the rich soil. Small gold and blue insects buzzed and spun about, birds chirped and dashed from branch to branch, and an occasional chipmunk or rabbit, upon seeing him, flung itself wildly away in silly panic.

If the committee were composed of members who held equal powers, thought the Maharal, then the temptation for corruption would be that much less. But for many years now, there had been a *primus*—a mayor. *Primus*—now that was a nice name, indeed! It was exactly the same word used in non-Jewish communities to designate the leader. Why did Jews love to imitate the gentiles? Did they find gentile culture so much more pleasing than their own?

It was perhaps understandable. The Jews were in exile, and the gentiles were the government, the kingdom, the armies, the royal palaces, the coats of arms, all the accoutrements of power. Vanity and emptiness. But on this earth, a human being needed air as well. So it was no wonder that

THE MAHARAL

some Jews were deluded by the pomp and power of the gentiles, no wonder that some Jews wished to copy gentile forms in order to find self-respect in their own eyes.

But to be so self-deluded! To seek such obvious imitation of the gentiles! This craze was hardly limited to Prague. Across Europe, there were communities that boasted that they were led by a Jewish bishop or a Jewish pope. That was the glamour that they wished to emulate.

Of course, Jewish history was full of Jewish leaders, so many recorded in *Tanach*. But the intent of the true Jewish leader was to be one with his people. It seemed all too obvious that the intent of these men was to stand apart.

The Maharal stepped over the fallen trunk of a huge tree trunk, amidst the still-standing trunks of younger, smaller trees.

Ah, but there was their error, he thought. The large tree had fallen, while the smaller, equal-sized trees had remained standing. Similarly, the man who set himself to rule as an individual separate from the community would lose the strength of the community, and he would fall.

In later days, the Maharal would write down this idea. "When a person acts like a royal ruler, separating himself from the community, he eventually becomes so separate that he does not consider himself a part of the community. It is well-known that anything that is separate does not have the strength that something connected to the whole does. For instance, water that stands by itself quickly evaporates, while water in a river encloses. Therefore, a person who rules and is separate from the community does not live long." (*Chiddushei Aggados*)

Here in the forest, thought the Maharal, one could see the order of nature. Every element—every leaf, every grass blade, every animal, the crawling insects and the mighty bears—all part of a whole, and each occupied its own niche. A person who sought power sought to leave his niche in the creation. Nor could one expect a human being to covet power without being harmed. The post itself was corrupting, brooded the Maharal.

He was to write, later on, "A political leader seeks his own glory and greatness, and not the glory and greatness of God, as is seen among various kings. It is impossible for a leader to be saved from this failing." (*Derech Hachaim*)

Why was this? It is the nature of every human being to, at times, influence others, and at other times be influenced by them. But when a person puts himself on a level where he would only rule over others and never let anyone rule over him, he violates his own nature, and that would inexorably lead to damage. "A person who is an imperious leader does not want to receive from the flow of life. The person who acts imperiously makes himself a leader over others and denies his capacity to receive." (*Derech Hachaim*)

As the Maharal continued his wanderings, his thoughts left the realm of the everyday and found their home in the ideal spheres of spirit and ultimate completion. He crossed from the forest onto the main road. Before him lay the royal city of Prague. To the side of the city were the well-ordered fields where wheat and vegetables grew, and in the midst of the city, the smooth and pure Moldova River poured endlessly. The Maharal slowly turned his steps back to Prague. Just as the purity of the river ran through the worldly concerns that the city of Prague represented, so could the Maharal find an ideal and pure core within government.

It was precisely out of an incomplete and corrupt world that *Mashiach* would come and bring the Jews their complete redemption, just as Moshe Rabbeinu had brought the redemption by coming out of Pharaoh's corrupt palace.

The Maharal later wrote these exalted thoughts in one of his *sefarim*: "The kingdom of *Mashiach* will emerge from a kingdom that precedes it. The holy Jewish kingdom that has a Godly and inner level blossoms out of an unholy kingdom. This is the fitting path for such a Godly and inner kingdom.

"In a similar manner, when a fruit is incomplete, it remains within the peel. Then, when the fruit grows and ripens, the peel falls away. This is because everything that has an inner level comes out of something that is exterior to it.

"Therefore, Moshe Rabbeinu grew up in the house of Pharaoh. The purpose in this was that the holy and Godly level that was in Moshe should emerge from the physicality [of his surroundings]." (*Gevuros Hashem*)

High, threatening clouds had been gathering, and a brisk, cool wind blew up, ruffling the tree branches. The distant clouds were briefly illuminated by a flash of lightning, and a few seconds later, thunder crackled through the air.

The Maharal gathered up his cloak and walked with strong, broad strides back to Prague. There were still storms to come, still much to do. But he knew that as imperfect as this world was, as difficult as the struggles were, it was precisely out of this imperfection and these struggles that the time of *Mashiach* would arise.

There was a sweet, intoxicating scent in the air. The fresh breeze blew more stiffly, bending the tree branches in the wind, and the excited birds rose and circled in the air. Even before the storm had come, one could already feel the freshness it would leave behind.

Two days passed. Then, on Tuesday, the king summoned Mordechai Meisel to the palace, where a high-ranking minister handed him a rolled page.

"His royal highness looks with favor upon your request to retain the committee of five rabbis," said the minister, speaking faintly through his nose. "But he has added in his royal reply, which you hold in your hand, the express condition that all elections held by the Jews of Prague be completely fair and that no favoritism at all be permitted to color their outcome."

Meisel lowered his head in shame. Matters had come to this: that a gentile king had to rebuke a Jewish community for their communal practices. But he left the palace joyful that the king had approved the request. Now the Maharal's program for cleansing the political process would be allowed to go on. Now there was immediate and concrete reason for all the Jews of Prague to give thanks to God.

13

The Iron Face

ANOTHER STORY IS TOLD ABOUT THE GREAT POWERS OF THE MAHARAL and the mysteries that surrounded his labors to bring Jews close to God. This story cannot be validated but is widely recorded. It demonstrates the Maharal's supernatural ability to probe beneath the surface of people and even inanimate objects.

The muscular young gravedigger swung back and forth rhythmically as he filled the small hole, while the two rabbis watched anxiously. There is a breeze, the sound of the earth thudding into the hole, and a clear, thin and sharply unpleasant odor.

The two rabbis turned away. "Thank you, Pesachiah," one of them told the shoveller, who was now tamping down the earth by walking back and forth over it.

"Most mysterious," said the other man, who name was

THE MAHARAL

Rabbi Asher. "I cannot understand it. You must explain, Reb Nosson."

"I suppose I should," Reb Nosson replied. They walked slowly back to the city as the sun glinted dully on the rooftops and the flowing Moldova River. "Yesterday, Mordechai Meisel called me to his office in the town hall, where he gave me a cloth bag from which a terrible odor came."

"The bag we just now buried."

"Precisely. He told me the following story."

As the two men walked slowly back to the city, followed by Pesachiah, his shovel slung across his shoulder, Reb Nosson recounted the story that Mordechai Meisel had told him.

Meisel had been sitting in the Maharal's *beis midrash*, where he often came to learn, when a young Jew in Polish garb had come in. A few heads looked up in curiosity but no great wonder. Jews were always coming from many cities around Prague to learn from or even just to speak to the Maharal.

The Jew came up to Meisel. "Excuse me," he said in a Yiddish whose Polish inflections sounded strange to Meisel's ear. "I wish to see the Maharal. I have been especially sent to present him with a new *sefer* of Torah thoughts." He mentioned the name of the author, a rabbi who was teaching at a prominent *yeshivah* in Luntschitz, a town in Poland.

"Come with me."

Followed by the nervous young man, Meisel walked through a door and into a hallway, at the end of which was the Maharal's private study. The door was ajar, and Meisel peered in to see the Maharal taking a small *sefer* down from a shelf.

Meisel knocked softly.

The Maharal turned around. "Yes?"

"I am sorry to disturb you, Rabbi Loew. There's a man here from the *beis midrash* in Luntschitz with a *sefer* that Reb Aharon has recently composed."

THE MAHARAL

"Please let him in."

The young man stepped up to the door and recited the blessing made upon seeing a great Torah sage, "Blessed are You, O God, our Lord, King of the universe, Who has given of His wisdom to those who fear him." He lifted up the cloth bag that he had been holding in his left hand. "I have come to give you this *sefer* that has been written by one of the outstanding rabbis of Luntschitz." Opening the bag and pulling out a *sefer*, he began, "On behalf"—but the room immediately filled with an over-powering stench that radiated from the *sefer*.

In fright, the Polish Jew let the *sefer* drop to the floor and his face turned white as paper.

"Put the *sefer* back into the bag," the Maharal commanded, "and carry it out of the *beis midrash*."

The Polish Jew remained frozen, so Meisel picked up the noxious volume, snatched the bag from him, stuffed the *sefer* into it and disappeared from the room. When he returned, the Maharal had opened the window and the Polish Jew was stammering apologies. "Rabbi Loew, I didn't mean—I never thought—"

The Maharal tried to speak, but the Polish Jew kept interrupting him. "I'm so sorry—what a terrible thing—who would have dreamed—"

"Compose yourself," snapped Meisel, and the young man fell silent.

"I am not upset at you," the Maharal assured him. "The odor was nothing that you could have known about. It was the odor of *avodah zarah*—idol worship."

"Idol worship?" gasped the young man. "Reb Aharon is a famous Torah scholar!"

"I have no doubt of that," the Maharal replied, "and I do not suspect his integrity. But something is amiss. Meisel, see that the *beis midrash* continues to run smoothly. I shall be away for a few days. Order a carriage for me immediately. I am

THE MAHARAL

on my way to Luntschitz to investigate this bizarre affair."

The Maharal drew a cloak about his shoulders and took hold of his heavy walking stick. "Hurry man, hurry," he urged Meisel. "There's no time to waste!"

Meisel hurried from the room. A carriage soon rolled up to the *beis midrash*. The Maharal stepped in and shut the little door behind him, and with a snap of the coachman's whip, they rattled swiftly out of Prague.

It took a number of days, overnight stays in meager roadside inns and many changes of horses before the Maharal's carriage lumbered into the broad and muddy main street of Luntschitz. The Maharal procured a room at the local inn and, stepping into the street, entreated a small boy with long sidelocks to point out the whereabouts of the *beis midrash* where Rabbi Aharon learned.

The boy, wearing ragged knickers, a slouching cap and *tzitzis* that dragged below his knees, volunteered to take the Maharal there himself. And so the dignified and tall figure of the Maharal followed the thin figure of the child leaping eagerly ahead and pointing the way.

Upon arriving at the *beis midrash*, the Maharal thanked the boy and entered the building. Most of the houses on the street were old and dilapidated, but the *beis midrash* was in excellent repair. Inside, the furniture was handsome, the walls were freshly whitewashed, and in a corner was a shining stove to heat the large room in the winter.

Though the Maharal was unknown to the men in the *beis midrash*, his distinguished bearing struck them so that they instinctively rose from their seats.

The Maharal, for his part, having glanced at the faces of the various scholars, strode firmly forward to where one particular scholar, with a snow-white beard and shining, innocent eyes, stood.

"Reb Aharon, I presume?"

THE MAHARAL

"Yes."

"I am Rabbi Loew. I had the pleasure of receiving your *sefer* a few days ago."

"Rabbi Loew!" exclaimed Reb Aharon.

"Sh!" said the Maharal. "I am here on a brief but urgent errand, and I do not wish my presence to be known. Let us sit a moment and talk."

They sat down at the table, and the Maharal leaned forward and asked in a confidential tone, "Tell me, Reb Aharon, who supports the *yeshivah*?"

"Reb Avraham."

"Rabbi Avraham? Who is he?"

"I thought everyone knew who he is. I guess his renown has not spread far beyond our borders. Such is fame, a moment of glory within a brief circumference. But I forget myself."

"Do you need a drink of water?"

"No, I was just going to explain. Reb Avraham is a wonderful man. An impoverished and hard-working Jew, two years ago he was blessed by God and began earning great sums of money. Being of a pious and naturally generous nature, he has been kind enough to pay for the building of this *beis midrash* and the payment of those of us who learn here."

"Hm," said the Maharal. "I must see Reb Avraham. At once!"

"It shall be my most happy duty to take you."

"No, thank you," said the Maharal. "I do not want to trouble you. But if you would be kind enough to point out the way, I would be most grateful."

Together, the two aged Torah scholars walked from the *beis midrash*. Rabbi Aharon pointed down the main street of the Jewish section of Luntschitz, which effectively constituted the only street of Luntschitz. He waved his hand down the road. "Go straight, all the way," he said, "and then ask."

"I'll do that," the Maharal promised.
"You can't miss it."
"It was a pleasure meeting you."
"The pleasure was all mine. Please come again."
"You are very kind."
"Not at all."
"Goodbye."
"Farewell."

With a final clasping of hands, the two men parted. Rabbi Aharon returned to toil in the fields of Torah, and the Maharal walked down the main street, taking care not to dirty his shoes on the long, muddy patches.

But soon the road was paved, and the shacks and shanties were replaced by substantial homes and then great wealthy mansions. Asking directions of an under-aged youth carrying a querulous goose under his arm, the Maharal was pointed in the direction of a large, white mansion whose shutters and trimmings were painted a light blue, giving the house a carefree, Mediterranean flavor.

The Maharal lifted the large, bronze door knocker and knocked at the door. A moment later, a young maidservant opened the door.

"Yes?" she inquired.
"Is this the home of Reb Avraham?"
"Indeed."
"Is he at home?"
"Who shall I say is calling?"
"The name is Loew. Yehudah Loew."
"A rabbi?"
"Yes."
"One moment, sir."

The maidservant slipped away from the door. From within, the Maharal heard a spirited conversation between a man and a woman.

THE MAHARAL

"I don't like the blue trimming on the house," came the woman's voice. "It makes the place look like a doll house!"

"But dear," came a deep, male voice, "it's very handsome. You'll get used to it."

"I wish you had painted it dark green. That looks more serious. I like dark green."

The Maharal was not able to hear the end of this conversation, because it was suddenly interrupted by the maidservant announcing his presence.

A moment later, a tall, burly figure came out to meet him.

"Not the famous Rabbi Loew of Prague?"

The Maharal bent his head in acknowledgment.

"Fame! What is fame, at times," said the husky, yet stately Jew, "but the crown that heaven blesses those who are its royal servants? But come in. How can I help you?"

Reb Avraham led the Maharal to his private library.

The two men sat down at a burnished walnut table, and the maidservant brought them tea and cake.

"Do you require my financial assistance?" Reb Aharon asked. "Can I help support your *beis midrash*? Or can I help an impoverished Jew?"

"I have just one question," replied the Maharal.

"Yes?"

"How did you make your fortune?"

"Ah!" Reb Avraham sat back in his chair. "That is a story that takes some telling. And as I do, have some cheesecake. My wife made it, and it's very good."

And Reb Avraham related the following tale:

Reb Avraham had been known for many years as Avraham the Junk Dealer. Old metal and rags were his stock in trade, and his figure, bent under a load of rubbish, was a familiar sight. Collecting here, gathering there, he would then go to the city, where he would sell his merchandise for the pittance on which he and his family subsisted. So his life went on year after year, as his tall form began to stoop over, but he never lost his good spirits.

One day, as Reb Avraham was rooting through a pile of discarded debris, he came across a piece of metal molded in the shape of a woman's face, serene and fair, whose eyes were two large sapphires. Reb Avraham gasped at their beauty. These were no simple ornaments but precious stones of incalculable wealth. He turned to the back of the face, and with a little stick, he prodded the metal. Beneath the grime, it was soft and yellow. Gold! This discarded face was worth a fortune!

Avraham the Junk Dealer considered. To whom could he sell it? None of the people with whom he dealt could afford to pay anything even close to its real value.

There was only one place where he could sell this face. Avraham had many misgivings about going there, but he decided that there wasn't anything wrong with doing so—at least, not too wrong.

The next day, Avraham the Junk Dealer paid a visit to the bishop of the local church. The church, Avraham knew, was a powerful and wealthy organization, and the bishop was known as a very rich man. The butler at the door turned his nose up at the sight of the Jew, but Avraham insisted that he had important business to discuss with the bishop that would take no more than a few minutes of his time. Appearing skeptical, the butler went off nevertheless to deliver the message.

Avraham was told to come back later that afternoon. He spent the day wandering in the street, and when he did return, he was admitted into the bishop's personal library. The bishop was a robust, corpulent man whose bald skull gleamed in the light of the sun that softly broke through the large, french windows opening onto a porch with a balustrade of Italian marble.

THE MAHARAL

"You are a junk dealer, are you not?" said the bishop. "Yet you say you have something of interest to display."

"Yes, I do, sir," replied Avraham. He extracted the face from his bag and handed it over to the bishop.

The bishop's face lit up. "Why, this is exquisite!" he exclaimed. "The workmanship is masterful. And the eyes—I will have to speak to a jeweler to confirm their worth, but they seem genuine and very costly."

"And if you please, sir," added Avraham, "the face itself is entirely of gold."

"Why, so it is," exclaimed the bishop. "I shall consult a jeweler and a dealer in precious metals. After they give their evaluation, I shall discuss the purchase of the face with you. Come back tomorrow at this time."

Avraham held out his hand, but the bishop said, "I shall hold this here for safe-keeping. Don't worry. Everything shall be done in order."

Avraham spent the night in any agony of worry. The bishop might simply keep the face and deny ever having seen Avraham.

The next day, when Avraham entered the home of the bishop, he was mortified to find a law officer there. "Now," said the bishop, "both this officer and I would be very interested in hearing where you obtained this precious object that you showed me yesterday."

It was clear that they suspected Avraham of stealing the precious face. But after a long questioning, they were persuaded of Avraham's innocence.

The law officer left, and then the jeweler and dealer in precious metals entered and gave their evaluations. Avraham was astounded to hear the high value that they gave it, far beyond what he himself had dreamed its worth could be.

"Very well," said the bishop after they too had gone on their way. "I am willing to pay you a fair price for it. You shall

THE MAHARAL

not say that we men of the church treat Jews unfairly." He named a price to which Avraham, overawed, at once agreed without even attempting to bargain. Without saying another word, the bishop opened a casket from which he counted out a large number of gold and silver coins, which he poured into a sack and handed to Avraham.

It was not long afterwards that Avraham was no longer called Avraham the Junk Dealer but Reb Avraham. Now he was a man of property.

This was the tale that Reb Avraham told the Maharal in his handsome library.

"Ah!" cried the Maharal, cradling his head in his hands. "For a bag of gold, you entered into transactions that reek of the taint of idol worship. Know, Reb Avraham, that the *sefer* of Reb Aharon that you sent me was permeated with the odor of that abomination!"

"Mercy!" cried Reb Avraham. "What can I do to seek atonement?"

"You can do the following. Wander from your home with only a bag of meager possessions upon your shoulder. Roam along the roads and through the towns of Poland and Bohemia in this way for a year, repenting and seeking in the course of your self-imposed exile God's care and forgiveness, which He shall surely extend to you."

With that, the Maharal stood up and left the mansion.

The next morning, after tearfully taking leave of his wife and children, Reb Avraham kissed the *mezuzah* and then, without a backward look, set out on his way, past the astonished passersby. Soon he was far beyond the town limits, a small figure trudging through his own exile.

"This was the story that the Maharal told Reb Meisel, and that Meisel told me," concluded Reb Nosson, as he and Rabbi Asher walked back to Prague. "And today we buried that very *sefer* of Reb Aharon."

THE MAHARAL

"It is quite extraordinary," said Rabbi Asher, "that the Maharal's sanctity is so great that in his presence, the uncleanliness that was inherent in the *sefer* could not conceal itself."

"Yes," interrupted Pesachiah, who had been closely following the story. "And if that is so about a *sefer*, how much more do the secrets of a human being reveal themselves to the Maharal?"

Neither Reb Nosson nor Rabbi Asher responded to Pesachiah's comment. But it is was many months before they again appeared before the Maharal.

14

Rebuke and Leadership

THE MAHARAL HAD THE OPPORTUNITY TO MAKE BLESSINGS OF thanksgiving over the course of the next years. His son Betzalel had a second son named Menachem. Soon afterwards, a third son, Yekusiel, was born, and then a daughter named Shlift.

One day during morning prayers, the Maharal was puzzled to hear a blessing of thanks made by one of the worshippers.

"Blessed are You, our Lord O God, King of the universe, who does good deeds for those who are in debt to Him, for having given me only goodness."

"Amen," responded the congregation. "May He who has done only goodness for you always continue to do so."

Why had Reb Zalman uttered this blessing, a blessing that one made after having escaped danger or having returned from a long journey? What had happened to Reb Zalman, a glass-maker who had not done anything more exciting than walk from his house to his shop and then back again?

After the prayers, Reb Eliyahu, one of the community leaders, walked over to the Maharal.

"Good morning, Rabbi Loew," he said. "Just see how pious even the common citizens of Prague are."

"What do you mean?" asked the Maharal.

"Reb Zalman. The one who made the blessing of *Hagomel* today."

"Yes?"

"On the way home from his work last night, some anti-Semite threw a stone at him and missed."

"And that is why he made the blessing?"

"Yes. It's rather touching, don't you think?"

The Maharal frowned. "Not at all. He is a pious Jew, but it is not for such things that our sages instituted the blessing of *Hagomel*. This is just like the recital of *Shir Hayichud* after the morning prayers."

"Rabbi Loew! Surely you are not opposed to that as well?"

"Yes, I am. These people mean well, but they are violating the intent of our sages, who said, 'It is forbidden to continue praising Hashem after one's prayers.'"

"But Rabbi Loew, this is their way of serving Hashem."

"But is it the *Halachic* way of serving Hashem?" replied the Maharal. "We may not push off the words of the sages because of the imaginings of simple people who think that such things will bring them close to God." (*Nesivos Olam*)

"You give strict rebuke," said Rabbi Eliyahu.

"Perhaps," said the Maharal. "But I'll tell you this. I will rebuke the people most of all for not accepting enough rebuke."

"You can be a hard man—with all due respect, Rabbi Loew."

"Do you think it is an easy thing to rebuke correctly?" the

THE MAHARAL

Maharal replied. "It is quite difficult. A person must first work on himself and be sure that there is nothing questionable in his own life and behavior. Then he has to learn the art of rebuke. One must be firm but also loving. One must tell the truth, but not in such a way that one will drive people off. One must begin by telling the person one is rebuking the good points one sees in him, but not to the point of servility."

"And yet, Rabbi Loew," Rabbi Eliyahu continued, "aren't you afraid that you may anger people? I have heard your rebukes. You speak out fearlessly against wealthy people who do not help support *yeshivos* where poor people can send their children. You speak out against the custom of referring to everyone as a rabbi, and you have called such rabbis 'sheep.' (*Megillas Yuchsin*)

"When a *darshan* came here last winter and came up with strained interpretations that you didn't like, you said that such *darshanim* are greater than King David, for King David had taught words of Torah that no one had ever heard before, whereas such *darshanim* taught words of Torah that no one had ever heard before nor would hear again. (*Derush Al Hatorah*)

"You have challenged judges and rabbis for being dependent on wealthy patrons and not rebuking them when they should be rebuked.

"Aren't you afraid that these same wealthy and powerful people may be moved to do you harm?"

"Let me answer you this way, Rabbi Eliyahu. There is one other characteristic that a person who gives rebuke must have. Like the prophets, he must be willing to risk everything—curses, insults and blows. Without such courage, there cannot be rebuke."

The Maharal's words were few and simple, but he said them with such deep authority that Rabbi Eliyahu had no more argument to proffer.

THE MAHARAL

Not all of the Maharal's public work involved controversy. In his walks, he was shocked to see the wretched houses in which the poor Jews lived: broken-down homes with moist and crumbling plaster, roofs of dried, split boards that let the rain fall through. Dilapidated fireplaces filled entire apartments with smoke and soot. Babies were sick and undernourished, and young men and women pale and anemic.

These poor souls slaved as porters, merchants and old clothes salesmen and often died in middle-age wizened as if they had lived a hundred years. And then, when they died, there was no one to take care of their funerals, and they left the world yet more impoverished than they had entered it, for they had entered with the love of a mother and father and the blessing of a congregation in the synagogue, and yet now they might leave friendless and bereft of the comforts and the blessings of a Jewish burial, of a *minyan* at the cemetery. Their relatives would be forced to beg for shrouds and some grudging cemetery workers would hurriedly dispose of the body of a Jew who had toiled on a shadowy and thankless street and then in poverty returned his soul to his Maker.

In 1564, Rabbi Eliezer Ashkenazi, seeing the sad state of the impoverished, had established in Prague a *Chevrah Kaddishah Gemilas Chassadim*, a relief organization that was dedicated to helping their plight.

Rabbi Ashkenazi had been a student of Rabbi Yosef Titzak in Salonika, Greece. Born in 1512, the same year as the Maharal, Rabbi Ashkenazi was a great Torah sage, a Kabbalist and a doctor as well.

The Maharal, building on the framework of this organization, expanded it and made it more dynamic and effective. Ultimately, it served as a model for similar organizations across all of Europe.

Now the water carrier had an address to turn to when his tattered garments could no longer shield him from the frozen

THE MAHARAL

January wind; the homeless wanderer had a bed to sleep in and a bowl of soup to eat before continuing his footweary journey; the weak, nursing mother was visited by women who cleaned her room, warmed her hovel and tended to the needs of her pulling child; and the aged man who had passed away could now be buried with care and dignity.

Another concern of the Maharal was to help Jews counter missionary activity. Surprising though it may sound, in many cities at that time you could see on a Sunday morning in the churches, Jews of all kind, rich and poor, men, women and children. All seemed uncomfortable, but a few looked calm, even humming softly to themselves. If you looked closer, you would notice that these people had cotton stuffed into their ears. They were compelled against their will to attend and listen to the sermons of the Catholic priests.

"Because you Jews have rejected the true religion of love," the priest was saying, "you have been cursed, damned, reviled and rejected by God.

"Because. . .

"Because. . ."

The Jesuits, an extremely powerful Christian order, had prevailed upon the rulers in various areas of Bohemia to force the Jews to attend church on Sunday mornings and listen to speeches on the "gospel of love" intended to persuade them to convert.

It was partially in response to this propaganda that the Maharal wrote and published *sefarim* in which he presented a complete view of life according to the Torah. Occasionally, he would obliquely counter Christian teachings by putting a special stress on such concepts such as "The people of Israel are called the children of God," and "Israel is God's first-born son."

In 1582, at the age of seventy, the Maharal published his second work, *Gevuros Hashem*.

THE MAHARAL

There were two odd facts about the appearance of this *sefer*. It was published not in Prague but in Cracow, Poland. And secondly, it was published anonymously. Why was this so? At that time, relatively few books were being printed in Prague. Perhaps the Maharal wanted his *sefer* published where it would be assured of greater circulation. And why was it published anonymously? Perhaps the Maharal did so as a matter of modesty. Alternatively, one could speculate that the Maharal's rebukes of the Prague community had made him such a figure of contention that for him to have printed his new *sefer* in Prague and under his own name would have merely fanned the flames of controversy.

Gevuros Hashem was a well-ordered *sefer*, discussing in separate sections *halachah* and *aggadah*. It contains a commentary on the *Haggadah*, and much of the remainder of the *sefer* also deals with *Pesach*. This order was new in *sefarim* of this type. In addition, the approach to each topic was also new: each sermon, or *derashah*, comprised a broad and encompassing explanation of the topic under discussion.

The *Akeidas Yitzchak* of Rabbi Yitzchak Arama was a possible model for *Gevuros Hashem*. Just as *Akeidas Yitzchak* was intended in part to provide the Jews with a handbook of Jewish thought to counter the influence of the Dominicans, so did *Gevuros Hashem* present an outline of Jewish thought. But *Akeidas Yitzchak* was more of a philosophically-oriented work. *Gevuros Hashem*, while discussing philosophical ideas, did so within a framework of concepts of the Kabbalah.

As the brilliant day of Spanish Jewry was drawing to a close, the *Akeidas Yitzchak* shone a few more brilliant rays of Torah to the Jews of that period. With *Gevuros Hashem*, the Maharal presented a guidebook of Jewish thought that was to shine on Central and East European Jewry at the zenith of their Golden Age.

15

Fighting Slander

IN 1583, RABBI YITZCHAK MELLING, THE CHIEF RABBI OF PRAGUE, passed away. Although no new candidate for the official post was named, the Maharal was a natural choice. Thus, it was no surprise that the Maharal was asked to give the *Shabbos Shuvah derashah*, the sermon given on the *Shabbos* that falls between *Rosh Hashanah* and *Yom Kippur*. Although not stated openly, it was clear that this would be an informal test for the Maharal and that if the community board members approved of his performance he would be approved as Prague's next Chief Rabbi.

But before this day arrived, three distinguished rabbis sought an audience with the Maharal to discuss a most disturbing issue with him.

"Rabbi Loew, a plague is sweeping through all the Jewish communities," declared the rabbi who had been chosen as

THE MAHARAL

spokesman, a short man with a trim, square beard that he smoothed down with a neat, clean hand on which the fingernails had been squarely cut. Behind him stood the two other rabbis: one, with silver-blond hair, and a squint; and the other, tall and thin, with a large head balanced above his narrow shoulders, looking funereal in his long, black caftan and tall, black hat, occasionally twisting his sidelocks behind his ears.

"Throughout Poland, Germany and Bohemia, thousands of Jews are being struck down," the little rabbi continued. "And the plague is hitting everyone, but especially the best families!"

The overweight rabbi joined in, "The rabbi's own family has not been spared...Someone has to find a way to prevent these sudden accusations against upright people!"

The Maharal grimaced. "You cannot think that I am indifferent to the tragedy about us. It is something I have tried to forestall for many years. Those of us who wish to end this suffering are many. When we unite and act forcefully and wisely, we shall prevail.

"Now this is what I plan to do..."

Where had this plague of insidious and vile accusations come from? It was born of a germ that had infected and at times destroyed Jewish communities over the course of hundreds of years. Now it had erupted again. Who could tell how much more damage it would do before it could be eradicated?

The cause of this particular outbreak was well-known. The very name of the plague came from a skin discoloration called *nadler*.

It had started in the Maharal's birthplace, Posen.

The story goes that it started when two poor orphans were going to get married. Each had wandered through the Jewish communities of Poland since they were small children, getting food and taking lodgings wherever they could, sleeping in barns, synagogues or fields, eating scraps and often sharing meals with families little better off than they. Each had struggled through the difficult childhood years, begging or doing some menial labor in return for a pallet of straw and a bowl of soup. Chaim had worked in the wheat fields, picked fruits, chopped wood, gone on errands and helped tailors and shoemakers. He had sold rags, carded wool, schlepped water and polished floors. And when there was no work to do and he walked along the long, dreary roads between towns, he would sleep in the fields and in the chilly morning drink water from a frosty stream, mumbling a few prayers he had learned by heart, and move on.

Devorah, too, had lived a life of want. Starting as a young child, she had travelled in groups of beggars, always hungry, pallid and crying, always grateful for a scrap of bread and leftover bones. Twice she had lain insensible and moaning with a terrible fever that had threatened her life. But at the end of each illness, she had arisen from the paltry bed that some townspeople had provided her, where the beggars had taken loving care of her and returned to her strength.

As she grew, she earned her keep by working as a maid, laundering clothing at the riverside, where she would rub the clothes with hard soap and beat them on a rock as she stood in the freezing river current. She sold the wormy apples that the farmers didn't want, took people's geese and chickens to market, helped the cook in wealthy homes, and sometimes, left without work and too proud to beg, she would go hungry, or be invited for a meal and a bed for the night by a kind-hearted family.

Both made their way to Posen, where they ended their wanderings. Chaim, who had always been fascinated by synagogues, by men praying and learning, had become the *shammash's* helper, and he also carried water from the well to the distant houses where Menachem Mendel the water

THE MAHARAL

carrier, his back hunched and his legs shaking, could no longer carry the heavy buckets.

It was here that, after a few months, an observant member of the *Gemilas Chassadim Chevrah* hit upon the happy idea of marrying off the two orphans, who seemed to have so much in common.

Chaim and Devorah both agreed, and the preparations for the marriage were begun immediately. The new couple would live in the attic of a crumbling, wooden house. Neighbors made food for the upcoming joyous occasion: large loaves of *challah*, beet soup, meat and sugar-dusted pastries stuffed with plums and apples. There would even be dancing, for two musicians, a fiddler and a drummer, had been hired to play for the price of a meal. Devorah's wedding dress, which had previously been the wedding dress of a dozen other orphan girls, was taken from its trunk, and a clever tailor with nimble fingers took it in to Devorah's size. Chaim was given a well-worn suit that one of the wealthy men of the town no longer needed. Chaim would take care of this well, for it would be his only *Shabbos* suit for many years to come.

On the morning of the wedding, Frieda, a grandmother with a thin, pointed face and merry eyes, who had spent many hours preparing Devorah for her marriage, came in with exciting news.

"My dear," Frieda said, brandishing a pair of scissors, "we shall soon have to cut your hair. But I want you to know that I just heard something from my husband that is a very good sign from heaven, my dear Devorah, about your coming marriage!"

Devorah was flushed with excitement. "What is it?"

"My husband just came back from morning prayers, and do you know what he told me? He told me that this morning, when he went to the *mikveh*—for he goes every day, he is such a pious man—he saw Chaim there, because today is your

THE MAHARAL

wedding day, my dear, I am so happy for you, you should only have joy and happiness and wonderful children who will grow and learn Torah! Well, my husband told me that he saw the most wonderful thing there, a sign that Chaim has been blessed by God from birth, and that you will have a very wonderful marriage, with many children and grandchildren who will take care of you in your old age, my dear, just as my own children and grandchildren are so good to me, even though I really do not need any help, thank God!"

"But what did he see?"

"Who, my dear?"

"Your husband? What sign did he see?"

Frieda waved a hand. "Oh, I'm coming to that, my dear. You needn't rush me. A story must tell itself. Well, my husband told me that he saw on Chaim's back a *nadler*—a birthmark—shaped like the letter *yod*, the letter *yod*, my dear. And later, after morning prayers, when he went and told the rabbi about this, the rabbi said that this was a wonderful sign from—but you're trembling, my dear, my dear Devorah, you're trembling, sit down, my dear, what's wrong? I'll get you a drink of water."

"I must go see him, right now!"

"But my dear, you don't know what you're saying. You can't go see him, it's your wedding day. You know, you have to wait until the *chupah*—"

Devorah stood up. "No, I tell you, I have to see him right away."

"But my dear, it isn't done. You aren't well, my dear Devorah. Perhaps you should lie down—"

With unexpected resolution, Devorah strode past Frieda and out the door as Frieda, expostulating, followed her and grabbed her elbow. But Devorah walked ahead, pulling her arm free.

Devorah strode down the street, her face white and

THE MAHARAL

drawn. Frieda stepped hurriedly at her side, out of breath, protesting, "Devorah, please, tell me what's wrong, dear girl. You must rest!"

Devorah walked up to the synagogue and boldly entered, and Frieda fearfully walked after her. "What's wrong, my poor thing?"

There was a handful of men in the synagogue, some dressed in *tallis* and *tefillin* and others in the process of taking them off. Some men were learning, and at the front of the synagogue, two men were standing and talking to Chaim, who had his back to the door.

"Baruch!" yelled out Devorah, and Chaim turned around.

"Devorah! What's wrong?"

"Your name is Baruch," Devorah said, frozen like a stone.

"True, I was Baruch as a baby," said Chaim. "But when I had typhoid fever, I was given the name Chaim."

"Baruch," Devorah said in an unearthly voice, "I am your older sister!"

There was a great commotion in the synagogue. Men came rushing up, gesticulating and yelling. Chaim himself turned white as plaster and said in a still, shocked voice: "Devorah? My older sister?"

"Baruch, when you were a baby, I used to give you baths. You had a birthmark on your back in the shape of a *yod*."

The news spread quickly through Posen. There was to be no wedding, for the bride and groom were brother and sister!

That afternoon, instead of a wedding feast, there was a banquet in thanks to God for averting a possible calamity and reuniting a brother and sister who had thought that they had no more family in the world. The fiddler and the drummer played as merrily as at a wedding, the rabbi came and made as impressive a speech, and the poor guests ate as enthusiastically as they would have otherwise, and even danced in equal celebration.

THE MAHARAL

But there were those whose hearts, soured by the long trials of exile, now sought joy in the humiliation. "Did you hear?" they whispered. "How contemptible! A brother and a sister nearly married one another! Isn't it a joke? Isn't it a scandal? The rabbis should be more careful about allowing anyone to marry?"

And when Chaim and Devorah went on the street, they were followed by jeers and whispers, and laughing, merry-eyed faces hidden behind windows and half-closed doors.

"*Nadler!*" these people would call out at Chaim and Devorah, *nadler* meaning birthmark.

But this was only the beginning. The word *nadler* became a way of casting doubt on any marriage and on the legitimacy of children. "Did you hear about the Feuersteins?"

"What?"

"I can't say."

"No, really, tell me."

Looking around, grabbing the other one by the arm and leaning over to him confidentially: "*Nadler!*"

"No!"

"Yes!"

And so the plague spread through Posen and beyond, until it became a game, a joke which left behind it the ruined reputations of families and destroyed relationships. "Buy something from him? Are you crazy? From that *nadler?*"

"How can you be engaged to her? Everybody knows that her mother is a *nadler!*"

The plague spread from Poland to Bohemia and Moravia until, the Maharal was to write, "all the young people in the city streets were accustomed to call each other by insulting nicknames and to insult departed holy men and, more than that, they not only endlessly insulted the dead but the living as well." (*Nesivos Olam*)

No one was immune from the slander. One day, the

THE MAHARAL

Maharal received word that rumors had been spread about his own son Rabbi Betzalel and his children. So widespread were these poisonous reports that even good people began to wonder if there might be some truth to them, and the Maharshal found it necessary to issue a letter defending the integrity of Rabbi Betzalel and his family.

Now, the Maharal explained to the three rabbis in his study what he intended to do about the awful plague of *nadler*. After he had finished speaking, the short rabbi said, "But Rabbi Loew, you cannot consider doing such a thing! You are liable to arouse opposition and forfeit the opportunity to be Chief Rabbi of Prague."

"I am not selling my integrity for the price of a rabbinical seat," the Maharal answered testily. "I have told you how matters stand. Do you concur?"

"Yes, of course, Rabbi Loew." And the three men quickly slipped from the room.

The days of *Elul* arrived. Early each morning, the *shofar* sounded in the synagogues after prayers, the raw, elemental blast calling on every individual to enter the realm where no speech existed but only complete awareness of standing before God. The sound of the shofar stripped away all of one's excuses; it sobbed and cried and turned one's heart to crying before God as a child cries before his father.

Still, there were those to whom the blast of the shofar was no different from the chattering of the birds, and these men remained busy with the thousand details of intrigue, jealousy and gossip. The Maharal watched all this with a careful eye.

The last week of *Elul* came. Before dawn, the men hurried to the synagogues, carrying their *tefillin* and *tallis* bags under their arms, while the brilliant stars shone in the sky and the weightless clouds glowed underneath from the light of the sun that still lay beneath the horizon.

In somber voices, the men said *Selichos*. Each man faced

his life as he had lived it over the past year. With what would he come before God in just a few short days, when God would judge him and determine his fate for the coming year? But still, there were those who read *Selichos* as if it were a childish prattling, and continued their trysts and machinations.

And finally, *Rosh Hashanah* came. For two days, the Jews of Prague prayed for long hours, pleading before the King of the universe, who would decide during these days who would be inscribed for life and who for death, who would be inscribed for health and who for illness, who for wealth and who for poverty. Rich and poor, learned and unlearned, they poured out their hearts before the Ruler of the universe and prayed for the day when all evil would be driven from the land and the mouth of all creatures would sing to God.

And yet again, there were those who, leaving the synagogue, thought not of subservience to God but of the pleasure of dispute and libel.

And now began the days of repentance between *Rosh Hashanah* and *Yom Kippur*. Each morning, the men hurried to the synagogue before the eastern sky turned violet with the dawn.

And finally, *Shabbos Shuvah* arrived. In previous years, Rabbi Melling had given the *Shabbos Shuvah* sermon, one of the handful of times during the year when the Chief Rabbi would give a talk to the people and discuss their spiritual status, rebuking them if necessary. But now Rabbi Melling was no longer alive. Everyone looked forward to hearing the Maharal. He was now an elderly man of seventy-one, for decades an acknowledged Torah leader in all of Europe, a profound thinker and a fearless rebuker.

The Alteneushul was packed. Although the first breezes of autumn had begun to blow, so many people were crowded into the synagogue that it had become stiflingly hot, and the large windows had been flung wide open.

THE MAHARAL

As the Maharal, tall and angelic, wearing his *tallis* that reached down to his knees, stepped up to the *bimah*, silence filled the synagogue. Even the children playing outside the synagogue were called in.

The Maharal began by speaking in general about the ultimate goal of man, his abilities, his purpose. Then, having described this ideal, he described the sins that keep a person from attaining these high levels and which, instead, cast him far downwards.

"First of all," the Maharal said, "there is false honor: the honor that a person thinks is due him, that he thinks he can acquire and scheme for. Here we are in this petty world, hundreds of generations behind us and who knows how many generations to come. Above us are spiritual worlds, level upon level, filled with myriad angels, and above all of these is God Himself.

"And yet we scurry across the face of this world, and instead of thinking what is true honor, what is true glory—that is, the service of God and the spreading of the light of holiness and goodness—we are drawn after the pleasures and honors of this world; our lives are drawn into the pit of worldly ambition and desire, into the trap of petty acts whose purpose is to raise ourselves over others, and to cast others down.

"What is the source of this state that leads a Jew to constrict his mind and bring quarrels into the world? The answer," said the Maharal, "is egotism. A person's sense of self can become so great that he senses only himself, his own needs, drives and desires. So distorted is a person's vision by this self-centeredness that he cannot acknowledge that others also deserve goodness. In his small-mindedness, he is afraid that any good that they possess might deprive him of what he desires for himself.

"Such a person becomes insanely jealous. He cannot bear that anyone should share the good that he has, and he plots to deprive others of their happiness and to accrue more false honor and possessions for himself.

"In their selfish pursuit of their interests," said the Maharal, "Such people have blocked off their awareness of God."

"But there are others who insult God in another way: by insulting the dignity of others.

"Every person has in essence, the *Chumash* tells us, a *tzelem Elokim*—an image of God. When one does not act with proper self-respect, which is very different from egotism, one insults one's own image of God. What is proper self-respect? It is the awareness of one's own values, one's ideals, one's desires to serve God by doing the *mitzvos* and doing good. But one is faced with the challenge of meeting others who are filled with egotism and jealousy. It is easy to be drawn after such people—but to do so is to become obsequious and servile. To do so is to forfeit one's integral image of God.

"And once one is drawn after such evil companions," the Maharal continued, "and one insults one's own image of God, what happens next? One begins to speak slander and gossip. By seeking to gain the approval of those egotists, one again insults the *tzelem Elokim* and insults Hashem yet further, for one takes the precious gift that He has given us, the gift that sets us apart from the animal kingdom, which is speech. Rather than using speech for holy purposes and for good, one uses it for unholy purposes, to sin and to create unhappiness and dissension.

"The true honor of a human being is to align himself with the honor of Hashem. The type of honor that expresses itself in egotism and slander is contemptible indeed. It is easy to say this in the synagogue. But what about in one's everyday life? Can one at that time withstand the temptation of joining others and engaging in these sins that remove a person from God and from the world-to-come? Can one then withstand the excuses and the rationalizations? Can one walk in the path of

THE MAHARAL

truth even when one might lose some so-called friends, even when one fears that they will turn against him? That is the true test. That is when a person really learns his level of refinement."

The Maharal paused. A child whined and his mother shushed him.

"There are those," the Maharal continued, "who engage in slander against kosher families. For the sake of their own small-minded pursuits, they sow a crop of lies and jealousy, and they look with gladness upon the bitter harvest of tragedy and broken lives. There are children whose pleasure it is to throw stones and smash windows. We punish them to teach them that this is wrong. Yet there are adults, respected adults, honored adults, who do far worse. They throw names at families and watch in glee as the families are broken. Such people must be named, exposed and prevented from practicing their evil pleasures.

"And in particular," said the Maharal vehemently, "I am speaking about those who employ the vile epithet, *nadler*."

There was a stir. The Maharal had gone from lofty generalizations to pinpointing a specific ill in the community. Everyone knew who he was referring to. Everyone knew who were the people who went about spreading stories of *nadler*. Some of those who were attacked looked about indignantly, others shamefacedly stared downward, and yet others gazed placidly forward, as if none of what the Maharal was saying referred specifically to them.

"How much sorrow, how much grief, how much tragedy and despair," the Maharal continued, "have been caused by those who take pleasure in destruction, wrack and ruin? This can continue no longer. From this moment on, it is forbidden to engage in such vicious rumor-mongering and, in particular, to use the word *nadler* to describe any individual or any family.

THE MAHARAL

"I am now going to call up ten of this city's leading Torah scholars," said the Maharal. One by one, he called out the names of ten leading sages. As each rabbi was called, he came up to the front of the synagogue, where the Maharal was standing. The *shammash* reached into the *aron kodesh* and handed him a *Sefer Torah*.

Soon, the rabbis stood in a row behind the Maharal, each with a Torah scroll in his arms.

"In the presence of all the Jews of Prague, in the presence of these ten rabbis, in the presence of the *Sifrei Torah* that they are holding," the Maharal declared in a mighty voice, "I hereby proclaim that from this moment on, anyone who is found to have described anyone else by the name of *nadler* will be excommunicated. No other Jew will be allowed to speak with him or do business with him. He will not be counted for a *minyan* or called to the Torah. He will be considered as utterly contemptible and outside the pale of the Jewish community until such time as he repents fully and properly. And if he protests and says that he will accept any other punishment, he shall be told, 'No.' Because you have insulted the members of the community of God, you shall now be cast from that community until such time as you prove that you are ready and fit to return.' So may it be."

"Amen, so may it be," repeated the ten rabbis.

The Jews in the packed synagogue watched this ceremony with awe, and many with a sense of relief. Finally, someone was coming to grips with this terrible problem. Finally, someone had the courage to risk his own position and reputation, not afraid that if he spoke up for others that he himself would be the next target of the smear campaigns.

But there were those who resented this action of the Maharal and viewed his actions as a high-handed vendetta against their power and wealth. These were the men who engaged in this calumny that the Maharal had outlawed. They

THE MAHARAL

were few but powerful, and they were so accustomed to their evil ways that they could not even now recognize the contemptibility of their actions. Instead, they only thought how to thwart the Maharal.

But the fearless action undertaken by the Maharal destroyed their grip over Prague. Families that had been shunned were again accepted within the community. Those venomous voices who had spread the poison of *nadler*-rumors were now afraid to speak.

The plague of slander still continued in other cities. But in Prague, the Maharal's drastic move stopped this evil in its tracks. The Maharal had demonstrated that he was not only a great thinker but a great leader as well.

16

The Maharal on Trial

THE MAHARAL DID NOT LET HIS CARES INTERRUPT THE FLOW OF HIS thoughts and insights, an approach to life that was vibrant, healthy and complete.

"One must keep away from worry," the Maharal said. "It is a low trait to worry [constantly] about being punished [by God]." (*Derech Hachaim*) Instead, a person must try to be constantly joyful. "Laughter and joy are in themselves good, for they are a sign of completeness." (*Be'er Hagolah*) However, one should not "fill one's mouth with laughter" in an unrestrained fashion. (*Netzach Yisrael*)

"When a person dances, he has greater joy, for his soul is in its complete power, and then joy exists." (*Be'er Hagolah*) A person should enjoy the beautiful sights of nature that God has created. (*Gur Aryeh*)

This world, said the Maharal, is not something one rejects

THE MAHARAL

in order to come closer to God. To the contrary, he wrote, "when a person is divinely inspired, he does not consider this world to be so low." (*Ohr Chadash*) "There is no imperfection in the order [of the world] at all," declared the Maharal. (*Gevuros Hashem*) "Created beings were created because they have good in them, for every species has within it goodness." (*Derech Hachaim*) But it is not enough for goodness to be locked up within itself. It must be given over to others. "It is no praise to find a person who is complete within himself, such as a wise man, a strong man or a wealthy man. Only when one gives to another is true completion reached." (*Gevuros Hashem*)

"Even evil," declared the Maharal, "comes from goodness.(*Derech Hachamim*) Even if evil is found to exist in the world, in the end it will be removed, until only goodness will exist, without evil." (*Derech Hachaim*)

One must love one's fellow man, declared the Maharal, for when one does not treat another well, one is showing that one's love for God is incomplete. "Man was created so that when he has the opportunity to do another a favor, he does so." (*Ohr Chadash*) For "the fact that a person loves others is the love of God as well. Whoever loves another, loves all the work of God's hands; and if he hates others, it is impossible that he loves Hashem who created them." (*Nesivos Olam*) A person needs a good heart. Only through a "whole heart" can a person reach divine inspiration. (*Nesivos Olam*)

And one must serve Hashem by abandoning oneself to Him: "To the extent that one does not have anything from one's own vantage point, one is ready to accept from Hashem." (*Nesivos Olam*)

One can serve Hashem with both love and fear, said the Maharal, but love is superior. "The source of love and fear is the same." (*Derech Hachaim*) But with "fear of heaven, even though one reaches a high level, one does not have this world

THE MAHARAL

as it is, nor the essence of the world-to-come as it is, because the level of fear of heaven is not complete in itself." (*Ohr Chadash*) So "one can cling to Hashem only through love." (*Nesivos Olam*)

Thus did the Maharal create a Torah view of the world based on a sense of health, optimism and well-being.

It is fortunate that the Maharal made good use of all the insights he gained, even from his misfortunes, for he was soon to suffer another disappointment.

In 1584, shortly following the Maharal's dramatic *Shabbos Shuvah* sermon, the Prague community board met in the town hall.

As the leaders engaged in a long and heated debate, an observer in the streets of the city could see, flying high above the town hall steeple, an eagle soaring until it disappeared from view.

Meanwhile, the board members finished their debate, took a vote and came to the conclusion that the Maharal was not to be their Chief Rabbi.

How could this be? How was it possible that this Torah giant, this leader of his generation, could be found to lack the credentials to lead Prague?

The Maharal had spoken out forcefully against conflicts. Was the Maharal himself seen as a controversial person, one whose rebukes provoked further dissension? Perhaps it was thought that the Maharal was too holy, too idealistic to engage in the day-to-day decisions of a Chief Rabbi, that he should be left rather to inhabit the ivory tower of the academic scholar. Perhaps they were afraid of a rabbi who was independently wealthy and would not be cowed by the lay leaders.

Perhaps it was the Maharal's strongly-worded ideas of Torah education that had made him unpopular. The Maharal was a sharp critic of *pilpul* and *chilukim*. But in the same city of Prague was the famous *yeshivah* that had been headed by

THE MAHARAL

Rabbi Yaakov Pollak. Perhaps they were upset with the Maharal's many attacks on the approach of their beloved teacher.

Or perhaps it was a confluence of all these different groups of people, each with its own resentments against the Maharal and disagreements with him. Alone, perhaps, many of these groups would not have opposed him. But possibly when a few people whose self-interests were threatened by the Maharal's forthrightness declared that he should not become Prague's next Chief Rabbi, then others, whose opposition was more principled, were persuaded to join their vote against him.

The Maharal was like that great eagle that had climbed the sky high above the Jewish town hall of Prague. A man of wonders whose awareness reached far beyond the boundaries of his time and place. Others could not appreciate him; when they looked upon him, they saw only as far as their vision, limited to the culture and milieu of their day, could see. And so they judged the Maharal not according to what he was, but according to the limited vision of their minds.

From this point of view, they were right. The Maharal was not fit for them, for the Maharal transcended the borders and conditions of the exile.

Soon after this vote, the Maharal knocked at the door only a few houses down from his. "Rabbi Loew!" said the young man who opened the door. "Do you want to speak to my father?"

"Please," replied the Maharal.

The teenager walked swiftly away. Was the Maharal imagining it, or did he sense some embarrassment?

A woman came to the door.

"I've come to give your husband my best wishes," said the Maharal.

The woman lowered her head and replied, "Thank you

very much. My husband will be ready to see you presently."

"I will wait."

Then she also walked off quickly—too quickly? Was she also uncomfortable?

A minute later, the teenager came back and led the Maharal to his father's study.

"Congratulations, Rabbi Yitzchak."

Rabbi Yitzchak Chayes looked strained. "Er, thank you, Rabbi Loew."

Rabbi Loew patted him on the shoulder. "It's awkward, I know." He sighed and strolled about the room. "Everyone knows that I was expecting to be the next Chief Rabbi of Prague. But the committee didn't pick me but you, my brother-in-law!"

"I know that you are many times more worthy than I, Rabbi Loew. Please forgive me if by my acceptance I have slighted your honor."

"Not at all. You were certainly right to accept. You are a true Torah scholar, and the city of Prague did very well for itself in choosing you. I am glad and proud for you."

"You are very kind, Rabbi Loew. I had been afraid that you would be offended—"

"No, no, to the contrary—"

"Particularly because I have been publicly opposed to you on the issue of learning *pilpul*. I thought you might suspect that I had joined up with those who have been against you because they feel they must defend the honor of Rabbi Pollack."

The Maharal smiled. "Don't let that worry you, Rabbi Chayes," he said. "In every community, there will always be the little foxes who make decisions on the basis of personal biases. But I know that you sincerely and objectively believe in the approach of *pilpul* and *chilukim* and that your opposition to me has been based on fighting for what you believe to be the best way of teaching Torah."

"Heaven is my witness that it is so!"

"Rabbi Chayes, I know that the committee had many good reasons for choosing you. You are of the Altschuler family, an old and respected family here in Prague and I am, after all, a newcomer. Your family has lived here for many generations. And who is not acquainted with the story that your ancestors took with them some of the stones of their synagogue from Provence and, when the Alteneushul was being built, placed those stones in its foundation?"

Rabbi Chayes said, "I have also been afraid that you would suspect that I was elected over you because I had made use of my family connections."

"Don't even mention it. I know you too well, Rabbi Chayes."

Rabbi Chayes picked up some papers and shuffled them into order. "Indeed," Rabbi Chayes smiled, "I am a man of the *beis midrash*, not a man of politics."

"Then let me give you this advice," the Maharal said. "There are many issues the community has to deal with. When you will be Chief Rabbi, you will often find that some board members disagree with you. Take care. Some people will disagree with you because they really believe that they are right and you are wrong. But there are others who will disagree with you on everything you do. They will always paint themselves as wronged, and they will ask you to make just one little concession to please them. Then, after you make that concession, they will seek yet another and another concession, until they have gotten everything they said they wanted. And then they will attack you even more strongly and make more demands.

"These are people who speak eloquently in the name of truth and justice, but who are only concerned with power for themselves. Their only point in opposing you will be to take

THE MAHARAL

the power that you have. Do not be afraid of them. When you know that you are right and they are wrong, do not let them persuade you to do anything that violates your conscience—not even a 'little thing.' Although you will never rid yourself of them, you will in this way strip them of most of their power. But if you attempt to please them by giving them a little of what they demand, you will find that you will only become steadily weaker.

"Be strong, Rabbi Chayes! Prague did well in choosing you as Chief Rabbi."

"Your words distress me, Rabbi Loew," Rabbi Chayes said. "But I am comforted that you will, at any rate, be here to give me counsel."

"I am afraid that will not be so," said the Maharal. "I have decided not to remain in Prague."

"Not to remain in Prague! But you have been here for twelve years, Rabbi Loew. There is no need to leave. You were the center of the city even when Rabbi Melling was alive, and you shall continue to be the center of Torah life here when I am Chief Rabbi."

"That is not why I intend to leave. I am afraid that my remaining here would be used by certain parties to foment controversy yet again. The fact that we are related, the fact that we have disagreed on *pilpul*, the fact that I was disappointed in the possibility of becoming Chief Rabbi and you were offered that post—all these will be used to create more dissent. For the sake of peace, I have decided to leave this city."

"But where will you go?" inquired Rabbi Chayes.

"I have received a letter a few days ago from the community of Posen."

"Posen? The city where you grew up?"

"Yes. The leaders of Posen have officially invited me to move there and become Chief Rabbi of the Polish exiles throughout the province."

THE MAHARAL

"Posen is also a city of greatness and Torah learning."

"Indeed," said the Maharal. "I have even heard that the Maharsha is considering opening a *yeshivah* there in the coming year. I would certainly rejoice to be in the company of such a Torah giant."

Rabbi Chayes put his arms about the Maharal's shoulders and pressed him close. "We shall miss you dearly."

"I will miss you too, Rabbi Chayes."

"Will you leave your children here behind you?"

"Of course, Rabbi Chayes, though it breaks my heart. After all, they are grown and married now, with their own families. I could not ask them to uproot themselves and travel with me."

"Then since you are leaving," said Rabbi Chayes, "let us sit and learn Torah together for a while, for it is the Torah that binds the souls of all Jews as one."

The weeks sped on. Rabbi Chayes was installed as Chief Rabbi of Prague with great ceremony, as the Maharal himself looked on.

And then, a little while after that, the Maharal and his wife took leave of Prague and set out on the long journey to Posen.

17

A Delayed Letter

THE DAYS IN POSEN BEGAN IN TRANQUILITY. HERE THERE WAS A special committee for morals, overseen by seven rabbis. Here there was a place where one could devote oneself to Torah more easily. Perhaps related to this, here there was greater poverty, and thus greater simplicity.

As the Maharal had heard, the Maharsha did indeed bring his *yeshivah* to Posen, and he and the Maharal were often in touch.

Meanwhile, the Maharal heard good news about his family. His daughter, Gitteleh, the wife of Rabbi Shimshon Brandeis, had her first child, who was named Betzalel.

His sons-in-law, Rabbi Yitzchak Katz, who was married to Feigeleh, became Chief Rabbi of Vienna.

Then Gitteleh had a second son, Shmuel. Later, Shmuel was to become mayor of Prague, following in the footsteps of

THE MAHARAL

his father. And in emulation of the Maharal, he learned the Rosh with especial vigor, and he was able to review the Rosh's commentary on the entire Talmud by heart.

Outside the *beis midrash*, the birds chirped cheerily. White wisps of cloud strayed across the blue firmament. Heavy wagons, loaded with produce, creaked on the way to the market place and the farmers waved their fists at their tired nags and swore lustily in the name of their saints.

Before the Maharal sat a woman with a chicken who wished to know if it was kosher. Outside in the hall that served as a waiting room, a Jewish trader and a Polish farmer were waiting to see him. The Pole, a barrel-chested hunchback with clever eyes and a thin, hooked nose, which he continually rubbed with a white, bony finger, had refused the Jew's request to settle the matter of a thousand bushels of potatoes before a *beis din*, a Jewish court. But he had agreed to come and accept the verdict of the great and holy rabbi who had gained such renown even in the houses of the non-Jewish neighbors.

And after these two cases, there were the community disputes. Although he had left Prague, he had not been able to leave behind him the mire of disputation. There were again quarrels, arguments, jealousies and the thousand and one unimportant things about which petty minds squabble.

Upstairs, Perl took care of the house. But despite her cheer and all her charitable activities, she was growing gray and wrinkled. When she would receive a letter from one of her daughters living in Prague, her face would shine and her eyes would regain their sparkle. The Maharal sighed. Not that he was sorry that he had left Prague to come to Posen—as he saw it, there had been little choice. But he was sorry because after four years in Posen, he and his wife had not found the happiness they had sought. The little cares of day-to-day life had ground away at them here as well. Because Posen and

Prague were trapped within the same exile, they were plagued by the same community problems stemming from small-mindedness.

The Maharal disposed of the dispute between the Jewish tradesman and the Polish farmer. The farmer, having achieved more than he had expected, left rubbing his jaw with a crafty leer and nodding his head at all the Jews in the courtyard.

But the Maharal was grateful that he could exercise a good influence. Not long before, the Jews of Prossnitz had written him and asked him to compose some ordinances, some *takanos*, similar to those he had written when he had been rabbi in Nikolsburg. It was gratifying to know that he had done good in his life, and that he had now inspired others to do good as well.

Oh, but sometimes it was wearisome, very wearisome! Where was the mail? He could answer some letters now before returning to his learning. The shelf where his *shammash* left his letters was bare. The Maharal stood up from his desk and stretched his long, thin figure. He was still vigorous and hearty, thank Hashem. For that he was grateful.

Miles outside of Posen, a horse stood alongside a broad, dirt road, tethered to a tree and chomping the thick grass at its feet.

Thrown down from the horse's back was a thick sack of mail. Beyond that, a young man lay on his stomach, propped up by his arms with his back to the road, watching in the distance a farmer and his men moving like small stick figures across a broad, green field beneath the vast canopy of sapphire sky. Occasionally they called to each other, and the young man caught the faint snatches of their voices.

This was a day! This was a life! He didn't deign to look back at the sack of mail that he had hastily thrown off the horse's back. Let the mail wait. Let everything wait. It was spring, it was beautiful, he was young and strong, and he breathed in

THE MAHARAL

the pleasant scent of the grasses, sighing in pleasure. He was just a poor mail carrier, but on a day like this, with all of nature spread before him, with the heavens above his head like a cap of azure and the sun shining like a vast and molten pool of gold, he felt himself wealthy beyond all measure, more wealthy than any crabbed old man closed within his four walls and counting out his golden coins.

Let the mail wait! Today, he, the letter carrier, was wealthy, and he would be here a while and breathe in the intoxicating freshness of the spring.

Inside the leather bag that lay cast at the feet of the horse, who pawed in irritation at a fly as he plucked at the stalks of grass, was a letter that had been carefully composed, gone over and agreed-upon by a committee, and the name of the addressee written in handsome script upon the envelope: Rabbi Yehudah Loew, Chief Rabbi, Posen, Poland.

"Dear Rabbi Loew," the letter read, "in consequence of the fact that the esteemed Rabbi Yitzchak Chayes no longer holds the position of Chief Rabbi of Prague, we would like to take the opportunity of respectfully inquiring if you would be interested . . ."

In the following weeks, other letters came as well, letters from the Maharal's daughters and sons-in-law, letters from friends and students, and a letter from Rabbi Chayes himself, telling the Maharal what had happened and urging him to return to his home in Prague.

One late evening, the Maharal told his wife, "Don't feel bad about what happened to your step-brother."

"Oh, I don't feel bad," his wife said, but in a dull and unconvincing voice.

"No, I mean it," replied the Maharal, putting a bowl of water with a metal cup in it on a stool next to his bed. "The fact that Reb Yitzchak was forced to resign his office was only a confirmation of all the good thoughts that I have had about him. Your stepbrother is a holy man, a Torah scholar. For him to descend to the level of communal politics, of intrigues and fights for power, was impossible. He just couldn't lower himself enough.

"As for me, Hashem has given me the strength to deal with such things. But that is not your stepbrother's role."

"You are right—as usual," said Perl. She gave her husband a melancholy smile. "But the fact is that he is planning to leave Prague and move to Prossnitz, and he is only waiting for us to return before he does so. Ah! Things must have gone very wrong. Poor Yitzchak." She sighed. "Hand me the *siddur*, please. I want to say the bedtime *Shema*."

18

Spring in the Air

"SOME PEOPLE SAY THAT THEY DO NOT UNDERSTAND WOMEN," SAID the courtier in his silver, laced jacket, taking a pinch of snuff from a silver box, "but that is nothing." He snorted the snuff up his nostril and sneezed with a polite hiss, then held the box out to the man with whom he was talking, who shook his head. "The real mystery—the real mystery in this world, my friend, is you Jews."

The other man, who was Mordechai Meisel, smiled at this.

"Our Scriptures tell us that we are 'a people who dwell alone.'"

"To dwell alone—that's all fine and good," expostulated the courtier, rolling his eyes about the large, gilded hall of the palace, as though seeking support for his words from the portraits of notables there. "And if you have some strange beliefs and customs, I do not suppose it is too difficult to understand them. But I am talking about the things you consider important. I mean your Rabbi Loew, for instance."

"Yes?"

"He comes back to Prague, a big to-do is made about him, and everyone is waiting for him to become the next Chief Rabbi. And what does he do? He says thank you very much, but he doesn't want the post. He'd rather sit at home and study his books. "So what do the Jews go ahead and do? They don't hire him to be Chief Rabbi, but they keep going to him anyway. I don't get it, I tell you. They want him, but he doesn't want them, but they still want him."

Meisel laughed. "It isn't such a great mystery. It's simply common sense."

"Exactly my point, my dear Meisel! What's common to you Jews remains extremely mysterious to us—what do you call us, eh? Am I a heathen or good enough to be a gentile?"

"You are a humorous old wag with a powdered wig and a very good appetite that will make your tailor rich, because he'll be having to take your jacket out again."

"It is the price I pay for my country, for I must eat at so many palace banquets," said the courtier with a grin. "But you haven't answered my question."

"It's really quite simple," Meisel replied. "When Rabbi Loew's brother-in-law lost the post of Chief Rabbi, Rabbi Loew returned to Prague after many of his family members asked him to. If Rabbi Loew had taken the post, he would have hurt the feelings of people in Rabbi Chayes's family, who are also part of his family. Besides which, he may not have wanted to be tied down to the public responsibilities of the post.

"As for the community of Prague, after they hadn't given Rabbi Loew the position four years ago, they realized their error and now they wanted to make up for it. So they now give Rabbi Loew the respect that he deserves. As I said, it's only common sense."

THE MAHARAL

"Common sense, yes, only to people for whom being good comes before being great."

"I suppose that Rabbi Loew is content to be king without a crown," Meisel added.

"And that's a rare thing indeed," the courtier replied, "especially when in these days there are so many crowns upon men who are not kings." He looked about him and added hastily, "Excepting King Rudolf, of course."

"Of course," answered Mordechai Meisel.

Indeed, the Maharal was the uncrowned king of the Jews of Prague.

And that spring, on *Shabbos Hagadol*, the *Shabbos* before *Pesach*, when the Chief Rabbi customarily gave a talk, the Maharal was invited to speak.

Once before he had spoken in a way that the townspeople still remembered vividly, threatening slanderers with excommunication.

But this talk was a talk of spring, of renewal, growth, hope and optimism.

The Maharal spoke of the meaning of creation, of God's rulership and of the ultimate turning of all people to Hashem.

"At this time of year," the Maharal said, "all nature rejoices: the grasses praise, the trees sing, all creation tells the praise of Hashem who manifests His presence through the beauty of nature. Even in the smallest creature one sees the praise of the Creator, for everything was created in order to give glory to the Creator of the universe.

"Hashem is the one and only God. As the verse says, 'There is no other.' (*Devarim*) But this verse means more. It means that there is nothing else but God. Hashem is so great, so vast, so complete, that although from our point of view we see objects and creation, from Hashem's point of view, nothing exists but He.

"And in such a world where all creation sings the glory of

Hashem who is so great that He is the only being that exists, what is the role of man?

"The role of man," said the Maharal, "is to connect himself and ultimately the entire world to Hashem, until 'He will be one and His name will be one.' (*Zechariah*) Hashem made the universe with order, with a set rhythm and purpose. It is the role of man to maintain and guard that order.

"Then even the evil inclination, the *yetzer hara*, is absorbed into the world that is connected to Godliness, and then the evil inclination becomes good. The evil inclination is necessary, for it was created in order to give a person free will. Therefore, the evil inclination completes the act of creation, and it is thus ultimately for the purpose of the world, which is good.

"The war against the *yetzer hara*," continued the Maharal, "is very difficult, and the battle is painful. But it is necessary. Ultimately, the people of Israel will win this battle and connect themselves fully to Hashem. But the Jews can do so only when they are united with each other, only when they love each other and help each other.

"Unfortunately, there are many things that prevent the actualization of this unity—the struggle to earn a living and the desire for political power among leaders, which cause bickering and division.

"But we must recognize that we are united with each other. We must acknowledge that brotherhood extends to all Jews, not just to those one would prefer to choose as one's fellows.

"Then, when a Jew learns that he has to love all Jews, when in his heart he feels affection for all Jews, *Mashiach* will come."

When the Maharal stepped down from the podium, he was greeted by warm appreciation. His message, which he had delivered for many years, was making its mark. It was not

THE MAHARAL

rank, prestige or wealth that was important in Hashem's book of reckoning. Hashem wanted to see Jews treating other with love, treating them fairly, doing favors for them, helping them, paying them fairly and on time, taking care of the orphan and the widow, seeing that the sick were healed and the impoverished fed. These were not simple acts of kindness but cosmic achievements that helped pave the road upon which *Mashiach* would walk to redeem the people of Israel and the world.

The Maharal returned to his beloved role of teacher. Again, he was in charge of the *beis midrash* in the Klaus Synagogue and spearheaded the effort for improvement in the method of Torah education.

19

The Magic Banquet

ANOTHER ONE OF THE LEGENDS ABOUT THE WONDERS OF THE Maharal tells of an encounter with one of the influential noblemen of Bohemia. This story is recorded in the book *Der alten Prager Juden friedhof* by Joszbeck.

"How long have we been learning together now, Rabbi Loew?"

"How long, Count Zoltan? I would say about five years."

"For five years, we have been learning the secrets of astrology and alchemy. And yet I hear that there are still greater secrets and wonders of which you are a master."

"I am a student of the Jewish Torah, which teaches us the commandments that every Jew must do to serve God. And since these commandments come from the Almighty, these are His greatest secrets, yet every individual can grasp them."

THE MAHARAL

"You are playing with me, Rabbi Loew. I do not mean such things as how to wash your hands in the morning, or what blessing to make on a piece of bread. Pah! Let us speak frankly. I refer to the secrets of the Kabbalah."

Rabbi Loew remained silent.

"I do not understand your belief in divine providence, Rabbi Loew. Look at me, a non-Jew, a count, a man who knows nothing of your Torah, nothing of your commandments." The count stood up and stretched his arm out at the green, rolling hills past the large windows through which sunshine streamed into the spacious chamber. "And yet God has granted me this great mansion with a magnificent view of the hills that roll all the way to Prague.

"And what has Hashem given you, the rabbi and almost king of the Jews, God's most obedient servant? You live in a small house in the middle of Prague. Do you have light in the summer? Do you have heat in the winter? Do you have even one-hundredth of what I have here in my castle—servants, stable of horses, farmlands, works of art, fox hunts, my pleasures and my might?"

"But I am happier with what God has given me."

"A suitably pious remark," the count said. He turned from the window and faced at the Maharal. "But tell me something, Rabbi Loew. One of my men, a most trusted servant, told me of something peculiar that he saw at your house when he visited the city last week."

"Really?"

"Ah, you are feigning ignorance, Rabbi Loew, but I shall speak plainly. He tells me and would swear that he saw four hundred of your students enter your small house. And when he dared afterward to come and look inside, bearing an invitation to come and learn with me, he saw that, as he had always seen before, there was not room there for forty, much less four hundred. Explain this if you will, Rabbi Loew!"

THE MAHARAL

"Is that what is troubling you today?" The Maharal laughed. "I assure you that your servant was not deluded, nor did he have any reason to fear."

"Do you then verify my servant's tale?"

"There is no need to do that, Count Zoltan. I invite you to come yourself, and bring your friends and servants. Tell them that they should prepare themselves to join me and my students for a royal feast. Bring as many guests as you will—even if there be two or even three times the number of my students, they shall still all fit into my house, where they shall be royally entertained. All I ask is that you let me know in advance when you are coming."

"Done, Rabbi Loew!" the count clapped his hand on the table. "Let it be next Tuesday, at six in the evening. I shall bring my closest friends and people who have high positions in the government, so do not let me down, Rabbi Loew."

The appointed day came. A handful of royal carriages clattered into the Jewish ghetto of Prague and pulled up before the home of the Maharal. It was a small, cramped building, its facade dim and stained with soot. As the count and his comrades descended from their carriages, they looked at each other skeptically. Was this where they were to be royally entertained?

"I hope," drawled one fat young nobleman in an affected accent, which entered the universe principally through the medium of his nose, "I hope, Count Zoltan, that you have not brought us here for vain purposes. My father would be most upset to learn that you had."

Count Zoltan, who owed this young nobleman's father some two thousand gold coins, was not cheered by the young man's insolent remark.

He walked up to the door and knocked angrily. If Rabbi Loew had played some outrageous joke on him, he would not take their previous friendship into consideration! Rabbi Loew would have to pay the full price. The door was opened by a student, and when the count looked inside, he gaped. He saw a lordly hall, a long, white-decked table about which sat the four hundred students of the Maharal, each one with a shining face, and far at the other end of the hall the Maharal himself at the head of the table, drinking from a golden goblet, with a few empty chairs near him.

"Come in," called out the Maharal. With unbelieving eyes, Count Zoltan and his party walked all the way down the banquet hall and sat down next to the Maharal. The walls were richly ornamented with portraits, a massive chandelier hung from the high ceiling, and on the table was china with exquisite blue and pink emblems. The drinking glasses were golden goblets, the cutlery was sterling silver, and food was brought in unceasingly from a farther room, on broad, silver platters.

When the count looked about, he saw that there were great double doors leading off in all directions to yet other wings and rooms, yet other halls and chambers, of this brilliant, great mansion.

The count and his royal friends were astounded. Here, in the cramped space of the Maharal's apartment, they enjoyed the luxury and splendor of a banquet that exceeded the greatest pomp of King Rudolf's royal dinners.

When the Maharal looked away from the table one moment, Count Zoltan signalled to his valet, pointing at the golden goblet that stood before him and gestured with his deep, black eyebrows; the valet, intuiting his meaning, grabbed the goblet and secreted it beneath his voluminous cloak.

After hours of rejoicing and feasting, the banquet drew to an end, and the Maharal accompanied his astounded visitors to the door.

They had almost forgotten where they were, and so they were again astounded when they stepped out into the simple street and, turning back, they saw nothing but the narrow house where the Maharal made his home. Wordlessly, the Count and his guests climbed into their carriages and travelled off to the count's castle, whose worth paled in comparison with the dazzling display they had just seen at the home of the Maharal.

Two days later, the count received amazing news. As he sat before the mirror in his boudoir curling his magnificent mustache, his valet stepped silently and announced, "Count Zoltan, I have news that I believe you will find of the greatest import."

Count Zoltan raised the bushy eyebrow above his quizzical left eye. "Indeed?" he said, laying down his ivory comb. "Speak!"

"The extraordinary news arrived that on Tuesday, at precisely the time that you had the honor to dine with Rabbi Loew, to which banquet I accompanied you, sir, the great castle of Lord Dershkvit, two hundred miles distant from Prague, mysteriously disappeared."

"Humph!" exclaimed Count Zoltan.

"Indeed, sir."

"And was there anything more to the news?"

"Indeed there was, your lordship. The servants report that the report has spread that the very next day the castle reappeared in its place. All its great treasures, its masses of jewels, its casks of gold, silver and precious filigree had been restored. Indeed, nothing had been harmed, misplaced or taken, except, sir . . ."

"Except?" With eager nervousness, Count Zoltan's hands gripped the dressing table before him until his tense knuckles showed white, and his eyes glared balefully at his manservant.

"Except, sir, a golden goblet."

"You don't say!" breathed the Count, regaining his composure.

THE MAHARAL

The valet stood at attention. "Will your lordship require anything more?"

"No, that is all. You may go."

With a wordless shimmer, the valet sidled out of the room.

"So that's it!" exclaimed the count, standing up and stomping about the room with barely suppressed excitement. "So that Rabbi Loew really does know Kabbalah! Ah, I'll get it out of him yet!" And muttering other such oracular sentences, he sat himself down again before the mirror to complete the care of his mustache.

The next day, Count Zoltan again sent for the Maharal.

When the Maharal arrived, Count Zoltan closed the door behind the two of them, leaning against it with his back. "So, Rabbi Loew," he exclaimed. "You have professed ignorance of Kabbalah. Well, after that little demonstration of yours last Tuesday, we can drop all pretense, can we not?" He gave a short, barking laugh. "Ha, ha!"

"Hm," the Maharal played for time. "Whatever do you mean?"

"Don't dissemble with me," cried Count Zoltan in rage. "Do you think I do not see? Or get the news? That banquet of yours. The disappearing castle of Count Dershrocken—"

"Dershkvit."

"Whatever his name was! All these add up to irrefutable evidence that you, Rabbi Loew, are a master of the secret arts of Kabbalah."

"And what about the missing goblet, Count Zoltan?"

Count Zoltan turned pasty white. "Ah . . . ah . . . you know about that, do you? Well, never mind, never mind! But now, as your long-time friend, I implore you to teach me Kabbalah!"

"I am afraid I cannot, Count Zoltan. It is difficult enough for a Jew to gain the high spiritual level necessary to learn this art in safety—how much more, then, for a gentile, for whom this wisdom was not intended."

"I demand it then from you as the count—Count Zoltan!"

"Even so, I am afraid I must refuse, with great regrets."

"I will not be denied!"

"Yet I cannot, your lordship."

"Cannot and cannot, you say. Yet you will, you will!" The count whirled about, and there was a terrifying gleam in his crazed eye. "Listen, Rabbi Loew. You know that I have great influence with his highness, the king." Count Zoltan stood at stiff attention, his face red and his shoulders rigid, and he clicked his heels smartly. Then he relaxed and resumed his pacing. "If you refuse me this, I shall see to it that the king will undertake the cruellest measures against the Jews. You know how easily he can be persuaded. You know how unstable his mental condition can be. Now, Rabbi Loew, what do you have to say?" And leering horribly, Count Zoltan glared at Rabbi Loew, twirling his left mustache between his manicured fingers.

The Maharal broke into a sweat. "You leave me no choice, Count Zoltan. If you insist so strongly, I will do as you desire."

"Good!" Count Zoltan kneaded his hands together in eager contemplation.

"But I have yet one request, Count Zoltan."

"Speak. If it is reasonable, I shall accede."

"To teach you the great secrets of Kabbalah could prove extremely damaging to you. Indeed, it could result in your death—if not worse!"

"If not worse!" repeated the count in a terrified whisper. "What shall we do?"

"This is what I propose, your lordship. A good friend of mine and a master Kabbalist is Rabbi Don Avraham of Saragossa. I propose to write him and tell him to come here to me. Together, I do not doubt that we shall have the wherewithal to initiate you safely into the utter mysteries of the Kabbalah."

"Very good," rasped the count. "Good day, then. My

servant will see you to the carriage. It is Thursday, and I know that you are eager to begin preparing for your Sabbath."

"Good day, your lordship," replied the Maharal and proceeded on his way distractedly. That whole night and the following day, the Maharal was in a turmoil.

"What ever will be?" worried the Maharal as he prepared his clothes for *Shabbos*. "If I summon Rabbi Don Avraham, will he actually come? Will he agree to teach Kabbalah to this count, even when I tell him the great danger that hangs over the heads of the Jews of Prague? Can I count on him? Ah, whatever will be will be!"

The Maharal finished putting on his *Shabbos* attire and was about to step out into the street to go to the synagogue, when there was a sudden clamor. The door burst open, and a swarthy man in flowing dress burst into the room and, throwing himself violently upon Rabbi Loew, wrapped his arms about him and kissed him on the cheeks in an Oriental fashion, shouting out excitedly, "Rabbi Loew, my old comrade, it is I, Don Avraham of Saragossa!"

"How extraordinary!" the Maharal stammered. "But listen, my dear friend. Let us go to the synagogue, and after the *Shabbos* meal, we shall talk."

Hours later, Rabbi Loew turned to Rabbi Don Avraham and told him, "It is more than extraordinary coincidence that you should happen to appear just when—"

"Just when you promised Count Zoltan that you would summon me and then both of us would teach him Kabbalah?"

"Exactly so!" said the Maharal. "How do you come to know of this?"

"Listen," announced Don Avraham, "and I will tell you of the great wonder the Creator has performed. Last night, as I lay upon my bed, there arose before my shuttered eyes a vision, and before my sleeping ears a voice did speak, for I dreamed that I saw you, Rabbi Loew, in an interview with

Count Zoltan, and he forced you to promise that you teach him Kabbalah on pain of the welfare of the Jewish people, and—"

"All right," the Maharal broke in. "So you learned through a prophetic dream what happened here last night. But my dear Don Avraham, by what miraculous device did you arrive here so quickly?"

"Well, I was just getting to that," Rabbi Don Avraham pointed out. "But I shall proceed with my narrative. Awakening from my sleep, I perceived at once that this was no ordinary dream but a prophetic inspiration. Immediately, I gathered a sum of money and a small sack of goods and set out to journey for Prague. Although knowing that this would be a journey of many weeks, I nevertheless trusted that—"

"Yes, so you began to journey," said the Maharal. "But that was only yesterday."

"I was getting to that," Don Avraham replied. "Suddenly, as I was walking down the street, a wind lifted me up. Although I moved my legs, I flew above the earth. All about me, houses, roads, farms, towns and cities flashed, as though they were no more than extraordinary illustrations, a fabulous phantasmagoria, and in this frightening and exhilarating manner, I was borne through city and forest, across lake and plain, sometimes wide awake, sometimes falling into a doze, constantly drifting, gliding, speedily traversing the many miles of foreign soil. And then, but twelve hours later, the great, strange movement stopped. My feet once again were walking upon solid earth. Once again I smelled the air. I felt the breeze. I heard the voices of those around me, and the panorama about me became sharp and clear. And when I asked where I had arrived to, those whom I questioned said to me that I was on the outskirts of the city of Prague. And so—"

"And so you are here."

"I am here."

THE MAHARAL

The very next day, the two giants of Torah travelled to the secluded palace of Count Zoltan.

The count received them with great honor, and after serving them fruit and water, he dismissed his attendant. "Now," he said, "we shall proceed to a secret chamber that I have prepared, where we shall learn the divine mysteries of the Kabbalah."

Through long hallways and narrow staircases leading downward, ever downward, the count led the two rabbis into the bowels of the castle, deep beneath the sunny rooms above, deep into rooms that had been carved into the living rock upon which the splendid mansion stood. At one point along the way, the count picked up one of a sheaf of torches that stood in the corridor. Dipping it into some inflammable liquid, he struck a flint and the torch sputtered into flame, and so they continued on their way. Finally, they came to a sealed door. The count fumbled in his pocket for his key, then opened the door and let the two rabbis precede him into the room. Once inside, he closed the door behind him and lit a number of candles that were standing in a candelabra.

The Maharal and Don Avraham looked about them. It was a peculiar and somber room, its walls hung with black drapes.

For a few minutes, the three men stood in absolute silence. The candles threw shadows on the solemn walls, and a rat skittered behind the walls.

Rabbi Don Avraham spoke. "So you wish to learn Kabbalah. Before we begin, Count Zoltan, I must make one thing very clear."

"Yes," said the count hoarsely.

"The Kabbalah is a wisdom rooted in holiness and in belief in one God. Thus, only those who are pure, only those who fear God, only those who do only good and who do not sin, only such people may enter its holy portals. Count Zoltan, can you tell me plainly that you are such a man?"

"Yes!" Count Zoltan spit out the word.

"Then, Count Zoltan, look about you."

Count Zoltan thought to protest, but the cantorial tone of Rabbi Don Avraham's voice awed him. He lifted his head and looked around him at the blank, draped walls.

And then he gave a shudder and a scream, for there, directly before him, was the living image of a young woman stepping forward, her face toward his with eternal sadness in her eyes. In her arms, she held a young baby, who fearfully gripped her dress.

Count Zoltan turned deathly pale and took a step back. "No!" he cried.

"Who is it?" demanded Rabbi Don Avraham.

"Father in heaven! It is my sister; my sister, and, and... her child."

With these words, the weird vision broke, and in place of the spectral woman and child there was only the black drape, only the flickering candle lights, only the skittering of a rat behind the walls.

"Your sister and her child, Count Zoltan?" continued Rabbi Don Avraham's implacable tone. "Be more precise, Count Zoltan, be more precise! It is your sister and *your* child, is it not?"

Count Zoltan could not speak, and he only nodded, almost insensibly.

"And they died through your hands!" concluded Rabbi Don Avraham.

Count Zoltan stood stock-still, as though he had been turned to stone. Then he cringed and began to plead before the two rabbis, sweat breaking out on his brow, "Yes, yes, it is all true. You know and God knows how guilty I am. But please, I beg you, do not reveal this secret, do not uncover my shame and guilt." He broke down and began sobbing. "Please. I will take you upstairs. And I—I shall not trouble you any

THE MAHARAL

further about the study of Kabbalah. Oh, it is true. I am far from being worthy of being allowed near that sacred science!"

We step back from this tapestry and see the mysterious, eerie sight of the tall rabbi, the exotic and oriental rabbi and before them the count, his handsome, young face distorted by an overpowering emotion, the candlelight reflecting weirdly on the somber, black walls.

20

Rumors in Moravia

BLACK CLOUDS RANGED ABOVE THE MASSED STEEPLES AND CROWDED roofs of Prague. Thunder clapped, lightning flashed madly, and the rain lashed downward in sheets that the wind drove against the sodden houses and the passersby fighting their way home.

The rain drummed against the latched shutters of the Maharal's home. Sorrow filled his heart now. Had this not been a time of joy? *Pesach* had been followed by *Lag b'Omer*, and, scant weeks after that, by the joyous celebration of *Shavuos*, the giving of the Torah.

But not long after, sad and sorrowful news had come to the Maharal. Just as Moshe Rabbeinu had gone up to heaven to receive the Torah on *Shavuos*, so had the Maharal's older brother, Rabbi Chaim, gone up to heaven on *Shavuos*—but he had not returned.

THE MAHARAL

The Maharal's grief was bitter indeed, and he felt keenly the loss of his brilliant, pious brother.

That year, 1588, the Maharal published his third volume and, using his brother's name in its title, he called it *Derech Hachaim*—The Way of Life, or, as it could be read, The Way of Chaim.

Derech Hachaim, a long commentary on *Pirkei Avos*, probed the Maharal's views on Kabbalah, as well as expressing his *mussar*, and other teachings.

In *Derech Hachaim*, the Maharal expounded the differences between philosophy and Kabbalah. These two, said the Maharal, were very different understandings of the world. Some years earlier, the Rema had published *Toras Haolah*, in which he explained the similarities of the Kabbalah and the wisdom of philosophy, which clothed some of the same teachings in a different language. Now, without mentioning either the Rema or *Toras Haolah* by name, the Maharal took issue with this view. He believed that Kabbalah and philosophy were worlds apart and that, faced with a choice between the two, he based his writings on the words of the *Zohar* and the other *sefarim* of Kabbalah.

The Maharal used many Kabbalistic terms in his works. And despite the philosophical language he sometimes employed, the Maharal clearly showed a Kabbalistic rather than philosophical point of view.

For instance, philosophy said that the names that describe Hashem (such as "Compassionate," "Mighty" and so on) are based on things that we see in the world around us and are borrowed to try to describe Hashem in a way that we can understand. But the Maharal disagreed and, arguing in the spirit of the Kabbalah, said that "such names are more than analogies." Rather, they "do not refer to the physical but to the abstract of the physical." Such names are actually describing traits that are in essence rooted in the upper world only mirrored in a lesser form in the physical world.

At times, the Maharal explicated the secrets at which the Ramban would only hint at. At other times, he showed that the words of our sages were not as easily understandable as they appeared to be, but hinted at deep secrets.

The Maharal did not insist that the words of the Talmud always be understood literally. Our sages said that the ram of Yitzchak has various parts: its horn was made into the shofar that blew at Mount Sinai; its hide was made into a loincloth for Eliyahu Hanavi; and its gut will make the strings of the ten-stringed harp that *Mashiach* will play. The Maharal pointed out that this statement is not meant to be understood simply at face value; it was rather, he said, emblematic (a *dugma*).

Even as the Maharal endeavored to assuage his grief for his brother's passing in the comforting waters of Torah, the roaring stream of controversy again caught him up in its foaming rapids.

"Now, our master, why do you not answer us and lead us?" read the Maharal from the letter that had arrived from Moravia. "Where is your zeal and might? Your great compassion and your awe over us have been held back."

Years before, Yisrael had been a student of the Maharal. He had been young but sharp and brilliant. The Maharal had guided and molded him until he had become an independent Torah scholar.

Then he had been called to fill a post as community rabbi in Moravia. He had gone there some time before, and fulfilled his post admirably.

Now he and the Jews of Moravia turned their eyes to the Maharal. Why did he not reply? Was he oblivious to their pain? Was he tired of the constant fighting? Did he see no advantage in healing wounds that were promptly torn open again? Or was he merely resting before his next entry into the fray of small-mindedness?

THE MAHARAL

Rumors were swirling through Moravia about a noted family, wealthy and with a good name. Perhaps this alone was enough to encourage and attract the evil eye of those afflicted by jealousy and an inner sense of poverty, those who, feeling empty inside, begrudge others their happiness.

Rumors spread of a strange and shocking history in this family's background. Years earlier, the great-grandparents of this family had lost their beloved, first-born child, an infant, in the confusion of a terrible pogrom, when each Jew fled in a separate direction to save his own life. The young, teenage parents had suffered further misadventures. The mother, Shaina, was struck on the side of the head and disfigured, and the father too was mercilessly pummeled. For many years, the couple lived in poverty, childless, the father constantly ill, the mother weak and pale.

Finally, the father passed away. His widow, now thirty years old, apparently unable to bear children and poverty-stricken, remained alone for several years, for whom would she find to marry her?

Yet she finally did find someone, a destitute orphan named Feivel many years her junior, in a marriage of two sad and broken people.

Yet to everyone's surprise, their union blossomed into happiness. The couple was deeply happy with one another. Shaina had a number of children and her young husband began to succeed in his business. Year after year, the children grew, and the business improved. Finally, they had a house full of noisy, happy children, and they were able to move out of their bedraggled shanty into a decent house. Feivel grew still wealthier, and they moved into a small mansion.

By then, it was time for their children to get married, and their father was so well-respected that they made very good matches.

And so, generation after generation, they had grown and

had become a very honored family in Moravia, known for their charity and kindliness. But perhaps it was this very reputation that attracted the attention of destructive and malevolent rumormongers. One of the offspring of the present family, Yerachmiel, was a dealer in wheat. He was not stern, and when faced with a customer who could not pay, he was always willing to make terms.

In recent years, he had begun dealing with a man named Alexander, a man who always complained of the troubles he was having, of his expenses, of family troubles that were eating up his income; and Yerachmiel always extended special credit and easy terms to him.

Slowly, precisely because Yerachmiel was so good and pleasant, Alexander began to resent him. How was it that he, Alexander, always seemed to be struggling, yet Yerachmiel was always doing so well that he could afford to extend a loan or reduce his profit? If Yerachmiel was so well-off, why didn't he make even better terms? Why didn't he completely overlook certain debts when Alexander had hinted so broadly that he was so hard-pressed?

One autumn, Alexander's daughter got engaged. While the rest of the family rejoiced, Alexander was filled with worry. After all, his family's only concern was to eat and dance at the wedding! His wife Miriam was already speaking of the beautiful, grand affair they would have that would put all their neighbors to shame and of the wedding gowns with fur trimmings that they would have made. But it was he who had to pay for it. And how deep did they think his pocket was?

Alexander went over to Yerachmiel and asked if he could take a loan on the collateral of a shipment of logs he was planning to sell that spring. Yerachmiel advanced Alexander the money, and Alexander went off, glad to be able to pay for his daughter's wedding after *Pesach*.

But in the spring, the market value of logs fell, and

THE MAHARAL

Alexander received much less than he had expected. Yet now, although Alexander had explained this all to Yerachmiel, Yerachmiel still insisted that Alexander honor his commitment and pay him back the money he had borrowed.

Alexander came out of their meeting fuming. It did not occur to him that Yerachmiel himself might be in need of the money. All he could think about was that which he was being eaten up by debts and hounded by wedding bills. This cheap, selfish miser Yerachmiel wouldn't give him a measly few more months so that he could pay off his debt, when after all, it wasn't his fault, was it, if the market for logs had suddenly lost its bottom?

When Yerachmiel began pressing Alexander, Alexander lost all patience. "That low-class cheapskate!" he muttered to himself. "People think he comes from such a high-class family. Well, I know one thing for sure. If his great-grandmother married some orphan who was hardly half her age, there had to be some funny business going on. I bet she accidentally married her own son, and that's why his family is so lousy cheap!"

From fevered muttering to himself, Alexander began bitterly reviling Yerachmiel and his family to all his friends and acquaintances. Within a matter of weeks, the rumor had spread throughout the community and been accepted as fact. The many descendants of Feivel and Shaina were all the unnatural products of a tragic, repulsive union. They were outcasts from Israel, and no kosher family should have anything to do with them, nor should anyone ever marry their tainted lineage.

When the members of this noble family heard these evil reports, they immediately protested and sought the authority of the greatest rabbis of their communities to put an end to the vicious slanders.

These rabbis swiftly issued public letters protesting the

THE MAHARAL

libel and denouncing those who engaged in it. But still, the rumors did not cease.

Rabbi Yisrael gathered these many responses together and mailed them to the Maharal. Perhaps he would be moved to act on behalf of this family and, by extension, on behalf of all those liable to be besmirched.

The Maharal read these letters. It seemed that all these protests from such great community rabbis did not suffice to end this pestilence. It seemed that he himself would have to enter the fray.

He wrote swiftly, remembering earlier controversies, sick at heart that such continued fights were keeping all Jews in the agony of exile and estranged from their Father in Heaven and from the coming of *Mashiach*.

Days after this letter came to Rabbi Yisrael in Moravia, it was being read from the pulpit by rabbi after rabbi in every affected community, and copies were widely distributed.

The Maharal repeated the condemnation of the other rabbis of this vicious slander, but he went even further than they in his explicit and forceful denunciation. "What an incredible thing," he wrote, "to create such a baseless falsehood that has no kernel of truth at all, a falsehood that is built on nothing more than anger, rivalry and a desire to ridicule others." The Maharal declared that he had "investigated [this matter] thoroughly and found the accusation to be a wicked lie based on manifestly false charges leveled by enemies."

Such was the charisma and moral authority of the Maharal that his epistle succeeded where previous protests had failed. Soon, the poisonous rumors died down. It was rather Alexander and those who had taken up his malicious talebearing who were now viewed with disgust.

21

Three Hundred to One

THE MAHARAL SLUMPED AGAINST HIS CHAIR AND SIGHED. THEN, shaking his head as though to clear it, he began learning Torah with fervor.

Outside, a priest in a long, scarlet robe stepped into a carriage and rolled away.

It was always the same, the Maharal thought. No matter how it started out, it always ended the same. Many non-Jews had come to speak with the Maharal. Some had come with set speeches, at the end of which they were convinced that the Maharal would convert to Christianity. Others would come with more subtle arguments. Still others, more open-minded, came to the Maharal with the intent of exchanging ideas. But it always ended the same way. They walked off disappointed although often awestruck by the great wisdom of the Maharal.

The Maharal could not refuse them. They were respected

THE MAHARAL

figures, figures whose goodwill was indispensable.

Another priest had now left. He had come to reason with the Maharal. He had come with the lessons and catechisms and logical arguments of his theology school and with the surety of his faith. But as the Maharal refuted his arguments and advanced his own position, the priest had begun to lose his temper. The Maharal had to tone down his replies. It was obvious that the priest was no longer interested in broad-minded discussion once the discussion was no longer under his control.

Such was the humiliated state of the Jews of that time. Entire communities were forced to attend harangues designed to persuade them to convert to Christianity. Great rabbis were forced into public debates on Christianity and Judaism, debates in which if the Jew spoke forthrightly he might be driven into exile for speaking vile heresy and, if he spoke softly, he was said to have lost the debate and payment of a sort was extracted from him or the community.

Oh, how wonderful it would be if a Jew were to turn the tables! How lovely it would be if a Torah scholar turned on his tormentors and challenged *them* to a debate! How splendid if, in this great and public debate, the Jew spoke proudly and firmly, thoroughly disgracing his opponents so that they had to slink off in shame!

With such rosy visions did the Jews comfort themselves and attempt to heal this most humiliating blow to their pride.

And in the midst of such ruminations, there arose, from scraps of fact and threads of fancy, such a story about the Maharal.

In the fourteenth century, there had been an earlier Maharal—"the first Maharal of Prague"—Rabbi Yom Tov Mauhlhausen. A great Torah leader and well-versed both in philosophy and Kabbalah, his fame rested on his expertise in such public disputations with Catholics. With self-sacrifice,

THE MAHARAL

he would travel whenever any community was forced to engage in such a disputation and serve as its representative. His most famous disputation was with Pfefferkorn the despicable apostate and hater of Israel.

He left a record of his proficiency in his *Sefer Hanitzachon*, in which he advanced all the Torah arguments in favor of belief in Torah as opposed to Christianity. This book was so powerfully reasoned that many Christians found it necessary to respond to it with their own writings.

One such person who responded to *Sefer Hanitzachon* was George Vitzli, who in 1544 published his *Dispute between Christians and Jews*. Vitzli arranged this book in the form of such a disputation, and the priest who presented the Christian arguments was Cardinal Sylvester.

Thus arose the idea that the Maharal disputed a cardinal named Sylvester. In 1910, a volume entitled *Chachmas Maharal* appeared in Pietrkov, purporting to be a record of this disputation, presenting a compilation of various statements that the Maharal had made in his many *sefarim*, arranged in the form of a disputation.

"You try my patience, Rabbi Loew," declared Cardinal Sylvester irritably. "I have brought you the most powerful proofs of the truth of Christianity. Will you never bend your stubborn Jewish neck?"

"These are not proofs," replied the Maharal, "for they are all logically weak, and they all ultimately depend on faith, a faith that I do not believe is warranted."

"You speak proudly now, Rabbi Loew," replied the cardinal. "But why do you sit here in your Jewish study hall in your ghetto? Do you fear to engage in meaningful dialogue with the sophisticated and enlightened graduates of our theological institutes?"

"I have borne too much insult!" declared the Maharal.

"And I can do so no longer. You have degraded the holy Torah long enough. I shall turn the tables on you, Cardinal Sylvester. In your theological school, there are three hundred advanced students and instructors, are there not?"

"Yes, there are, but—"

"I challenge them all—all three hundred—to a debate. Let the debate take thirty days, so that none can claim that he did not have the time to discuss adequately any issue that he wishes to. Let this debate be undertaken in public, so that all can see how three hundred Christian scholars fare in a disputation with one old Jewish rabbi. Do you agree to such a forum, Cardinal Sylvester?"

"Do I agree? I am most delighted. Your Hebrew arrogance has at last gone to your head, Rabbi Loew. You shall fail and either leave in disgrace or, if you possess the integrity, you shall abandon your superstitions for the tenets of the true religion."

At these words like barbs, the Maharal seethed inside, but said only, "Arrange the debate, and I shall be ready."

The day of the disputation arrived. Everyone, Jew and Christian alike, was in a great fluster, especially the Jews, who had much to fear should the Maharal be deemed to have lost.

Surrounded by a retinue of distinguished rabbis, the Maharal entered the great auditorium where three hundred priests sat in white tunics, each behind a lectern on which rested his learned notes.

The rules of the debate were set, and then, one by one, each priest stood up and engaged the tireless Maharal in debate. Cardinal Sylvester sat and watched eagerly, and many other notables looked on.

The Maharal, a tall, old man, stood behind his lectern and engaged each of his opponents in passionate and lengthy debate. The Maharal quoted from tens of sources by heart, astonishing those who watched, and his endless energy also

THE MAHARAL

astounded them. How long could the Maharal drive himself on?

One day of debates ended, and another day began. Then that day, too, drew to a close. Servants brought in tapers and illuminated the great hall with hundreds of candles, and the debate went on. And early the next morning, the disputants were in their place again. Only on *Shabbos* and Sunday did the disputants rest.

At times, the Maharal was forced to refute the accusations of the priests: the charge that the Jews killed the founder of Christianity; the cruel blood libel that Jews used the blood of a Christian child in making *matzah,* the alleged perfidy of the Jews. The Talmud was impeached, the rabbis accused of being blind and stiff-necked, their statements declared to be impious and willfully wrong. The Bible was quoted, verses taken out of context in attempts to prove that they were prophesying the coming of the founder of Christianity.

To all these, the Maharal responded eloquently, refuting every charge and demolishing each argument.

And then, the Maharal himself had the chance to go on the offensive. With great skill and brilliance, he pressed the priests on the many striking logical inconsistencies within the Christian bible, the "New Testament." How could the founder of a religion of love tell his followers that he came "not to bring peace but the sword"? How could the spokesman for compassion tell them to abandon their fathers and mothers who remained loyal to Judaism—that they should "leave the dead to bury the dead"? And there were so many contradictions in the very basic story of what he had done and what had happened to him. It didn't seem that any sense could be made of the many versions of the story that appeared in the text. But most of all, the Maharal said, how could Christianity have, claiming to be based on the Jewish Bible, created a religion in which a man is worshipped as a god?

THE MAHARAL

To all these questions, the priests, of course, had answers prepared. But the Maharal demolished these answers, showing them to be weak as a house of cards.

By the end of the thirty days of debate, the priests were in disarray and thoroughly routed.

Cardinal Sylvester was so deeply impressed by the Maharal's victory that he went to escort the Maharal as he arose and walked proudly out of the auditorium.

Cardinal Sylvester later sent a report of the debate to King Rudolf. King Rudolf was profoundly intrigued, and he devised the plan of summoning the wise and brilliant Maharal to his castle where they might speak together.

22

The Rabbi and the King

THE GREAT WHEEL OF LIFE ROLLS FORWARD, AND THIS WHEEL BRINGS with it sorrow as well as joy, death as well as birth. In 1591, the son of Rabbi Yitzchak Chayes, the Maharal's brother-in-law, died in Prossnitz. Grief came and then ebbed away, for one cannot live a life steeped in reminiscences.

Time passed on, and a year later, a stirring event took place in the life of the Maharal, an event that stirred the imagination of all European Jewry.

In 1592, four years after his return to Prague, the Maharal had an audience with King Rudolf II.

For years, no details of this meeting existed. Rabbi David Gans, student of the Maharal and historian, recorded merely, "In 5353, 3 *Adar* [February 23, 1592], Rudolf called for the Maharal. He spoke with him privately, like a man speaking with a friend. But no one knows what they discussed."

THE MAHARAL

From the brevity of this report, one gets a sense of the Maharal's great reserve. Although he had been granted one of the greatest honors that could be given to him by the king, he said not a word of it for the many years that followed.

One also gets a sense of the great awe in which the Maharal was held. Rabbi David Gans, a student of the Maharal, merely reports that nothing is known about the meeting. It seems that Rabbi Gans was too respectful to approach the Maharal and question him about the meeting. If the Maharal chose to say nothing, then that was the end of the matter.

Years later, however, more details were discovered regarding this interview. Inside a *Mikraos Gedolos*, an edition of the *Chumash*, was discovered the handwriting of the Maharal's son-in-law, Rabbi Yitzchak Katz, in which he reported on what he had witnessed of the Maharal's meeting with King Rudolf.

"On Sunday, the tenth of *Adar*," he wrote (thus differing by a week with Rabbi Gans), "in the year 5352 since the creation, King Rudolf relayed a message, by way of Prince Berthier, that Mordechai Meisel and Yitzchak Ben Chanoch Weisel should bring my father-in-law, the *gaon*, our master, Yehudah Leib, to the palace of Prince Berthier.

"Rabbi Loew came, taking along with him his brother, the outstanding *gaon* Rabbi Sinai, and myself...."

The Maharal, his brother and brother-in-law were also accompanied by a number of other prominent Jews. When they arrived at the luxurious palace of Prince Berthier, a servant came to the door and ushered the Maharal, Rabbi Yitzchak and Rabbi Sinai into reception rooms, while the other rabbis remained in the entrance hall.

The servant led the three men deeper into the palace, going from one room to another. They saw that each room had several entrances, and so it was possible for the king to meet them by walking through the palace via another route.

THE MAHARAL

Finally, they came to a room where the servant bade them stand.

Moments later, Prince Berthier entered the room from yet an even more interior chamber and greeted them.

With great respect, Prince Berthier bowed to the three men, walked over to them and gave each of them his hand.

"You are most welcome," he said. "Please be kind enough to follow me."

Prince Berthier led the three men into another room and invited them to sit on chairs that had been specially prepared for them. Although among Christians it is a sign of respect to remove one's head-covering, Prince Berthier insisted that, in keeping with the Jewish custom, they not remove their hats.

The three rabbis sat down, and the prince remained standing before them. He spoke to them about various topics, demonstrating the greatest respect for them.

Then Prince Berthier walked into an adjoining room, where he had his servant arrange two chairs to face each other. One chair was quite magnificent, and the other smaller and lower. Behind these seats hung a curtain.

Prince Berthier returned to the room where the three men were sitting and requested that the Maharal accompany him to the room with the two seats. Seeing this, Rabbi Sinai and Rabbi Yitzchak made as if to leave, but Prince Berthier stopped them and insisted very politely that they remain seated.

Rabbi Sinai and Rabbi Yitzchak sat down again, able to see and hear what went on in the adjoining room.

Prince Berthier had the Maharal sit on the tall, magnificent seat, and the prince himself sat on the other, lower seat. The prince began speaking in a clear voice, asking questions of the Maharal, which the Maharal answered. The two men spoke so loudly that it was possible for both Rabbi Sinai and Rabbi Yitzchak, who were sitting about eight feet away, to hear every word of their conversation.

THE MAHARAL

Apparently, the prince spoke this way on purpose so that the king would also be able to hear the conversation.

At one point, there was a sudden hush, and then the sound of chairs scraping. King Rudolf, who had been behind the curtain, entered the room. He himself put a few questions to the Maharal on the same topic that Prince Berthier had been speaking, which the Maharal answered. The king then went back behind the curtain again.

The Maharal and Prince Berthier spoke a bit more, and then they arose. As they walked back into the room where Rabbi Sinai and Rabbi Yitzchak were sitting, the prince held the Maharal's hand in his, and he spoke to the Maharal with great humility.

Prince Berthier then shook hands with the three men, showing them great respect, and accompanied them out of the palace and into the courtyard.

In his report, Rabbi Yitzchak described what the Maharal and the prince or the king discussed as *nistaros* (hidden things). He added, "As to what the topic was, it is fitting that it be concealed for the present, which is the custom regarding any royal matter. If God will give us life, in the right and proper time, we will reveal all these matters."

The following day, Prince Berthier reported that both he and the king had been very favorably impressed with the Maharal.

In later years, various stories circulated about what the Maharal and the king had talked about.

Perhaps the most reasonable supposition is that the king, having an interest in spiritual and mystical matters, had heard of the Maharal as a great Kabbalist and had wanted to discover something in this area. It seems from the interview with the Maharal that the king wanted to ask the Maharal a few specific questions, which he did through Prince Berthier, and that the king stepped out to elucidate some points.

THE MAHARAL

Did the Maharal himself engage in practical Kabbalistic activities? A hundred years later, the Chacham Tzvi reported that it was well-known that the Maharal made use of "divine influence." It is known, of course, that the Maharal's writings are heavily influenced by Kabbalah. More than that, he himself discussed what sort of activity one may engage in.

The Maharal taught that sorcery, which is forbidden by the Torah, consists of "engaging in supernatural rites that make things appear or disappear" (*Be'er Hagolah*), or that allow one to attain wealth or power. Also, one is forbidden to make use of a creature in a way that is not desired by Heaven. Therefore, it is forbidden to consult an *Ov* or *Yidoni*, for this involves consulting the dead, and the dead are meant to be in the other world and not this world. (*Be'er Hagolah*)

On the other hand, there are things that one is allowed to do. For instance, the Maharal taught that "it is a great wisdom to teach a person how to protect himself from [spiritual] destructive forces." (*Be'er Hagolah*) These techniques should be used only for the purposes of "self-protection and saving others." (*Be'er Hagolah*) One may also induce a non-physical being to "tell or show one something. Since this involves no action that is out of the ordinary, it is not considered sorcery. One connects oneself to a non-physical being in a manner that does not cause one damage." (*ibid*) "This," the Maharal explained, "used to be accomplished by binding a non-physical being by an oath in the Name of God, like one who makes a witness swear in God's name to tell him something." (*ibid*) "One is allowed to bind an angel with an oath, for at times, this is one of the purposes for which the angel was sent into the world." (*ibid*)

The Talmud teaches of some rabbis who used the *Sefer Yetzirah* "to create a fatted calf." (*Sanhedrin* 65b) This is permitted, for "the mentioning of names in *Sefer Yetzirah* is like any other prayer. When one calls out to Hashem, Hashem

THE MAHARAL

nullifies the decree against oneself. This is an accepted practice among the wise men of Israel." (*Be'er Hagolah*)

Is it possible that the Maharal created a *golem*? For one who believes in the incredible abilities of our holiest rabbis, the answer must be that it is certainly possible. The rabbis of the Talmud are said to have engaged in such practices. In more recent days, Rabbi Chaim of Volozhin, prime student of the Vilna Gaon and a very sober observer, testifies that the Vilna Gaon himself said that he had begun to construct a *golem* in his youth but, feeling that it was not the wish of Hashem, ceased the project.

Did the Maharal construct a *golem*? There is much about the Maharal that remains hidden and unknown. Therefore, this is not a fair question to ask. One can ask, rather, "Are the stories told about the Maharal's creation and use of a *golem* reliable?"

The first chronicler of the life of the Maharal was his student, Rabbi David Gans. In none of his writings does Rabbi Gans make mention of a *golem*.

The next chronicler is Rabbi Meir Perles, a descendant of the Maharal who in the early eighteenth century wrote *Megillas Hayuchsin*. Although he tells a good number of tales about the Maharal, he too makes no mention of a *golem*.

The first known mention of a *golem* made by the Maharal is in *Sippurim*, a collection of tales by L. Weisel, printed in Prague in 1847. In his introduction, Weisel says that he is retelling folk tales that he had heard old people tell. He tells the story of the Maharal creating a *golem* to help him in his housework. It seems hard to credit that the pious Maharal would make use of Godly powers simply to create a labor-saving device.

Then, in 1909, the collection of tales entitled *Niflaos Hamaharal* was published. Only now, for the first time, appears the link between the *golem* and blood libels; only

THE MAHARAL

now, for the first time, appear all the tales of Thaddeus the renegade priest, of a palace with haunted, secret passageways and of the other details which are so well-known.

There are several questions that the text raises.

First of all, one may wonder why such sensational events escaped being recorded before that time.

In addition, there are some peculiarities in the text. The manuscript is said to be an authentic diary written by Rabbi Yitzchak Katz, the Maharal's son-in-law. But the place names used are not the Czech names that Rabbi Katz would have used, but rather Slavic names, names that might have been more familiar to someone else in a Slavic country.

But most suspicious, the text contains gross historical inaccuracies. For instance, the Maharal is said to have engaged in his hypothetical debate with Cardinal Sylvester and immediately afterward been admitted to an interview with King Rudolf. This is said to have taken place in the first year of the Maharal's coming to Prague, in 1572. But Rudolf II did not become king until 1576! (And even then, he did not establish his primary residence in Prague until 1583.)

Niflaos Hamaharal is said to have been found in the Metz library by Rabbi Chaim Scharfstein and sold by him to Rabbi Yudel Rosenberg, who published it. Considering the above evidence, it seems reasonable to assume that both these men were victims of a clever forgery. The late nineteenth century was a time during which a number of gifted writers—among them literary *maskillim*—took advantage of the great interest in stories of *chassidic rebbeim* to create collections of tales out of whole cloth. Perhaps *Niflaos Hamaharal* itself was such a work, the brilliant creation of a man who wished to express his literary talent while laughing at the gullible Jew who accepted his work with simple piety.

But of course, none of this has anything to do with whether the Maharal actually did create a *golem* and, if he did, what he used it for. All it says is that the published stories that do exist about the Maharal's *golem* appear to lack authenticity.

The legends of the common folk of Prague were very certain that they knew exactly what the Maharal had discussed with King Rudolf. This is their version:

Under pressure from his wife and the bishop and church leaders who influenced her, the king signed a terrible punitive degree against the Jews of Bohemia.

"Well done, my dear," said the queen in a gravelly voice.

And the bishop added in an oily tone, bowing and squeezing his hands together, "Your majesty may be proud of this day, of this moment, of this great accomplishment!"

King Rudolf raised his tragic eyes and looked upon the company grimly, his forehead high, his lower lip forward of his upper lip and his chin thrust forward pugnaciously beneath his trimmed and curled beard. "I fear what may come of this," he exclaimed. "At times, I feel such hatred for the Jews that my blood boils, and yet, at other moments, I feel such felicitous affection that I cannot stay my passions, and I consider that they may be no less worthy than any of us."

"Your majesty," interrupted the bishop, "you need not fear the righteousness of what you have accomplished today. The people are with you and God, too, is with you."

"Yes," added the queen. "When Bohemia shall be rid of the pestilence of the Jews, you will see that all your affairs shall improve, and your horoscope shall show that the crown will rest upon your head in glory and command."

"Strange, strange, passing strange," murmured the king to himself. "But I had thought—perhaps it was a dream, or who knows what phantasm of a memory—that I had never married in my life. Yet here I have a queen, and she is most prodigious, thereto!" King Rudolf stood up heavily from his throne, and

THE MAHARAL

the crowd fell back before him. "I have signed this decree of expulsion of the Jews, but I feel faint, I feel weary, make way, for the king would fain lie down."

The king's courtiers swept along ahead of him, past the simpering bishop and the retinue of other notables, opening before the king the doors that led him to his royal sleeping quarters.

And even as the king walked with a heavy tread along the shining floors of the palace chambers, in another room some miles away, in small and modest chamber, strode a tall and impressive figure, bearded, somber and reflective.

The Maharal had learned through senses of the mystic arts about the base conspiracy of bishop and queen, and his spirit had travelled and witnessed the signing of the evil decree against the blameless Jews of Bohemia. And now, what could he do? The Maharal opened a Kabbalah *sefer* and studied its cryptic text deeply. He sat engrossed in this study, motionless, his eyes directed solely to the page before him, and his mind and soul soared into the higher regions and accomplished mysterious things.

King Rudolf lumbered into his luxurious bedroom and commanded his servants, in a drunken, sleepy voice, "Get out, poltroons!" Stripping off his crown, his ermine robe and other royal appurtenances, fell heavily onto the eiderdown quilt, and moments later, he entered a deep and strangely motionless slumber.

But in his mind's eye, the king was not motionless at all. He saw himself awake and refreshed, riding in his carriage. The sky was bright blue, the air warm but fresh, and he was feeling virile and serene. The carriage was going along a broad white road that led along the bank of the Danube River. The river flowed peacefully, and along the banks grew tall, handsome trees. As far as could be seen in either direction, besides King Rudolf's own retinue, no one was in sight.

THE MAHARAL

"Stop the carriage!" King Rudolf called out. The coachman reined in the four horses, and the carriage's large, red, wooden wheels rolled to a halt in the white dust of the road. Rudolf stepped from the carriage. "Wait here. I do not often have the pleasure of seeing the Danube River. It will give me pleasure to go for a swim."

"Yes, sir."

King Rudolf went off the road and past a copse of leafy trees that shielded him from view. He placed his royal garments upon the mossy ground and then plunged into the water, swimming with powerful strokes into the midst of the river, whose smooth current barely hampered him. Ah, what a pleasure! King Rudolf could feel the vigor in his body. He revelled in the cool water that caressed him and in the warm sun upon his back.

Swimming out some distance, Rudolf paused in the water and floated peacefully, turning back to gaze at the shore. But what did he see? Someone was standing at the riverbank, bending over his royal garments. King Rudolf's carriage and servants stood waiting on the road, unable to see the man through the group of trees.

"Hey!" Rudolf shouted. "Stop that man!" But his servants did not hear him and did not move.

Filled with wrath, Rudolf swam quickly back for the shore. Meanwhile, the strange man started throwing Rudolf's clothing over his own. "Help, stop, servants!" Rudolf called out, but no one heard him, and the man continued without even looking up.

As Rudolf finally approached the shore, the man, by now fully dressed in Rudolf's clothes, had calmly walked away from the river to the imperial coach.

"Wait!" the king called out, climbing up the bank, dripping wet, and running to the road. But the impostor had already climbed into the carriage, the coachman had snapped

THE MAHARAL

his whip, and even as Rudolf stepped onto the road, the carriage was disappearing into the distance. Rudolf ran after the carriage, but the sharp stones on the road cut his bare feet, and he soon gave up. And so he was left all alone in the forest, abandoned and unclothed.

Wearily, Rudolf trudged along the road, until he came to a small village.

"Help me, help me!" he cried out desperately. "Help me! I am the king!"

His cries attracted a group of villagers, but to Rudolf's surprise, they only jeered at him. "The king, eh? Strange king to be wandering about the forest with no britches on, eh?"

"Please, good villagers, I shall reward you handsomely."

"Oh yeah?" replied one of the men. "With acorns and wormy apples, I'll warrant!" And all the men burst into loud guffaws.

Rudolf grew wrathful. "I am your monarch. Show some respect, you fools!" But at this, the men grew even merrier and began poking at him. "Bow down, I say and show me honor!" roared Rudolf.

"You wants some honor, do you?" one of the men said. "We'll show you some honor, your royal highness!" He picked up a branch and struck Rudolf with it. "I'm just a swattin' the flies off your royal shoulder, your honor!" he said, and the other men roared with laughter.

Rudolf angrily rushed at the man, but the other villagers grabbed him and, beating him soundly as they joked about his mad pretension, drove him back onto the road.

Rudolf roamed from village to village, and in each village, the people jeered at him, pummelling him and sending him on his way. Rudolf ate berries and drank from ponds. Occasionally, a kind villager would give him some bread or cheese to eat, and finally, one man gave him some tattered rags to wear.

Rudolf lost his way stumbling from village to village, and

he finally wandered into the forest, growing wild and peculiar. Now villagers feared the sight of him, for he seemed an uncanny, frightful being. Months and years passed, and Rudolf became a strange hermit, living with the forest animals, eating fruits and game that he caught with his bare hands. The soles of his feet became tough as leather, his hair grew wild and clumped in elf-locks, and his fingernails and toenails grew long and hooked, as he wandered through the forest, skirting the villages, lost and miserable.

One early dawn, after many years, as he stumbled through the woods, he came upon a broad, white, dirt road that ran along a river. He dimly seemed to recall that he had been here once before. Walking swiftly upon this road—for now the sharp stones did not hurt his feet at all—he saw before him a great and marvelously beautiful city. He stared in amazement at the wondrous sight, until he realized that this was Prague, the city where he had lived, the city where he had been . . . the recollection came back hazily to him—where he had been king! And he began to recall with increasing clarity all that had happened to him, and he recalled the power and the glory that had been his.

Now, as he glanced down at his filthy, tattered clothing, his dirty body, his bare black feet, his hair flowing down his head, his wrinkled, dirty hands with long, ugly nails, he burst out weeping at what had happened to him.

He quickly made his way up the road until he entered the city. To his surprise, he saw no one there. The streets were empty, as though the city had been deserted. Without thinking, Rudolf strode firmly along, as though his feet knew where they were going. He passed by many streets and avenues, past great mansions without pausing to consider.

Now he was passing smaller houses, and then he walked through the gate of a large wall that surrounded part of the city. Even as he walked through, Rudolf recalled that he was

THE MAHARAL

entering the Jewish ghetto. And now, he grew confused, and he did not know where to turn.

In his despair, he pounded at the door of one of the houses on a narrow lane. An old, white-haired Jew opened the door.

"Let me in," Rudolf said in a hoarse, unclear voice.

It had been years since he had spoken with anyone. The Jew let Rudolf in and gave him a hot drink. As Rudolf sat, he began telling the man who he was and all the things that had happened to him.

Finally, the man replied, "I cannot help you, but I would advise you to go to the house of the great Rabbi Loew. He will be able to tell you what to do."

The old Jew accompanied Rudolf to the door and told Rudolf how to get to the Maharal's house.

Again, the streets were eerily deserted. Rudolf found the Maharal's house and pounded on the door. The door was opened by a tall, holy man. Rudolf was struck by the Maharal's aura, but he came in and began to repeat his story to the Maharal.

"I know all this," said the Maharal. "An impostor has come and is sitting on your throne."

"But how can I get back my crown?" Rudolf whimpered.

"This is what you should do," the Maharal replied. "This morning, the impostor is going down to the river to swim. Do to him as he did to you. When he has swum a good distance off in the water, go and put on his clothes, and return to your royal carriage."

"But look at me!" wailed Rudolf. "Look at my wild hair, my long nails! How can I go back this way?"

"I will take care of that," the Maharal replied. The Maharal took a pair of scissors out of a drawer, and he cut short Rudolf's hair and sheared off his long nails.

The king, now much relieved, hurried down to the river bank where he himself, years ago, had gone for a swim. He saw his royal carriage, his four horses, his coachman and servants. He hurried through the trees and saw, just where he had left his clothes years ago, the heap of royal clothing that the impostor had put down. Far away in the river, he could see the head of the impostor above the water. Quickly, King Rudolf put on the royal garments, and he hurried back to the carriage, even as the imposter, noticing him, shouted out and began to swim hurriedly to shore.

Rudolf walked onto the road, and his servants snapped to attention. Quickly, Rudolf stepped into the royal carriage.

"To the palace, and hurry!" he commanded.

"Yes, sir!" replied the coachman, and he raised his long whip and snapped it.

And with the sound of that snap, King Rudolf suddenly awoke, to find himself lying in his bed. Groggy and disoriented, King Rudolf struggled to sit up. The river, losing his clothes, being beaten and wandering in the forest for all these years—it had seemed so real. King Rudolf took a deep breath. Thank God, it had been no more than a nightmare. He had never had such a vivid dream before: coming back to Prague, meeting that Rabbi Loew, cutting off his hair and nails. What a relief that those horrible memories were a mere vapor and fantasy.

King Rudolf looked up at his night table and gasped in shock. There, upon the table, was a silver platter upon which lay a pile of matted, dirty hair and long, horny fingernails!

King Rudolf rushed out of his room. An uneasy servant looked out to see what was happening, and the king snapped at him, "Don't just stand there, call my advisor Ferdinand!"

"Yes, sir!"

When the royal advisor Ferdinand came hurrying, King Rudolf met him with, "Tell me, Ferdinand, have you heard among the Jews of a Rabbi Loew?"

Ferdinand looked curiously at the king. "Yes, your royal

THE MAHARAL

highness, the rabbi has achieved a certain fame as a wonder-worker and mystic."

"I must see him," Rudolf said. "Immediately."

"If your highness so desires, it shall of course be done."

"Then do not hesitate. Go!"

And that was the reason for King Rudolf's famous meeting with the Maharal.

In the course of that meeting, the Maharal explained that all these wondrous things had happened because of the king's decree of expulsion against the Jews. He warned that the king might suffer worse if that decree were allowed to go into effect.

Deeply moved, King Rudolf promised the Maharal that he would rescind the decree. He sent the Maharal home and called for the document that he had signed. Summoning the queen and bishop, he destroyed it in their presence.

"I shall not be intimidated by anyone into making decrees that are not for my good and for the common good," he spoke brusquely. "Great is the rabbi of the Jews and great are his mystic powers. From this day forth, I shall learn wisdom from him, not from those who seek to manipulate me and agitate against the blameless Jews!"

23

Out of Prague

"SURELY YOU ARE NOT LEAVING US, REBBETZIN LOEW!"

"I am afraid so, Malka."

The two elderly women sat together on a balcony that looked over a small garden in the back of the Maharal's house. They were close and old friends, as were their husbands, the Maharal and Mordechai Meisel.

"But I don't understand, Rebbetzin! After all the honor Rabbi Loew received not even two months ago, when King Rudolf saw him. Why, all of Prague is still talking about it."

"Yes, it was a great honor, Malka. But my husband talks about the greater honor of Torah."

"You were in Posen just four years ago, weren't you?"

"Yes, this will be the second time I go there. It is my husband's birthplace, as you know."

"But what is making him move so suddenly?"

THE MAHARAL

"It is really a bit of a secret," said Perl, "but we have been friends for so long, I am sure that I can tell you."

"What is it?"

"My husband has been invited to become Chief Rabbi of Posen and all of the Polish exile."

"How wonderful! *Mazel tov!*"

"Thank you, dear. You're very kind."

"I wish you the greatest happiness. It seems that Rabbi Loew feels that he can accomplish more in Posen than he could do here."

"Yes, that is what he said to me. He is eager to be in the rabbinate again, to improve a community and an entire country, and you know, he is particularly so interested in putting into effect all his new ideas on how people should learn Torah.

"Yes, my husband has often mentioned that to me. He says that your husband, Rabbi Loew, has been quite upset that people haven't really listened to him here. I must say, you and Rabbi Loew are really quite adventuresome to begin such a new move at your age. After all, if I am not mistaken, Rabbi Loew is already eighty years old, *keyn ayin hara*, and you are—"

"I am doing quite well, thank you. Yes, we are no longer young people. All of our generation is passing away. Poland had the Rema and the Maharshal. But now they are no longer with us. Perhaps my husband considers that Poland needs someone of the old generation."

"But what shall we do here back in Prague? You know, we have all come to take having Rabbi Loew for granted. It will be hard not to have him here with us."

"My husband has already thought of that. He has asked Rabbi Mordechai Yaffe, an outstanding Torah scholar, to come and take his place here."

Malka Meisel laughed. "That is interesting. Rabbi Loew

THE MAHARAL

goes from Prague to Posen, and Rabbi Yaffe comes from Posen to Prague!"

"Yes," said Perl reflectively. "That is the way it works out. But really, he originally came from Prague—just that he left when the Jews were expelled in 1561."

"I shall miss you terribly," said Malka.

"And I shall miss you as well, my dear. We'll write to each other!"

"Yes," said Malka. "But it won't be the same as having you here and sitting here with you like this. And you are going to leave behind all your children and grandchildren, my dear."

"Yes, that is true," said Perl. "But you know, I did so before. And we can always visit each other on holidays. It might need a little getting used to—at first. But in my life, my husband's teaching of Torah has always taken first place."

"Yes, you are so right, my dear. Last time you were in Posen, you only stayed there for four years." Malka smiled. "I hope you don't think me selfish if I hope that you come back as early this time?"

Perl squeezed Malka's hand affectionately. "Whatever Hashem decrees is for the best."

And so the Maharal and his wife again set out for Posen. In his very first talk in the Posen synagogue, delivered on *Shavuos*, the Maharal set out his program and expectations as the Chief Rabbi of all of Poland. The Maharal discussed the special nature of the Jewish people, who alone were willing to accept the Torah, and he talked about related matters dealing with the holiday of the giving of the Torah.

From here, the Maharal went on to say that he would make a new arrangement of general ordinances, particularly regarding the advancment of education—something that he had always yearned to do.

"In the last few years," declared the Maharal, "I have risen like a lion to try to improve matters. But unfortunately, I have not succeeded, for the people of this generation have refused to follow me.

"I wrote to the communities of Poland and Russia to make changes in the educational system, but that too did not succeed."

"I instructed people to teach their children *Mishnah* first and afterwards the order of learning as our sages taught us. But here too, I failed. Indeed, as long as the famous Torah leaders, whom the youngsters imitate, themselves do not learn *Mishnah*, then I declare in the Name of Hashem that there is neither Torah nor good deeds in Israel!

"I have demanded that the *rebbeim* teach according to the ability of the students and not try to force them to learn everything at once. But again, I was completely ignored.

"What a tragedy! The young people have hearts like archways and they are ready to take in the entire Torah. But in the end they are lost, and they become like the rest of the ignoramuses.

"But I am as strong now as I have been in the past, and I hope that perhaps my words will make an impression on those whose hearts have been touched by Hashem.

"Young people, do not be fooled! Take my counsel and follow the advice of the sages of the Talmud." (collection of quotes from *Derush Al Hatorah*)

In addition, the Maharal showed in this talk that he valued all members of the Jewish community. He spoke about the important role played by those who work for a living, about craftsmen, about the important contribution of the Jewish woman in supporting the household and bringing up the children.

The Maharal pointed out to those who are learned and who are engaged in business that they should not interfere in the work of the Chief Rabbi, for "it is impossible that they should remain dedicated experts in Torah while they are also devoted to their business concerns." Instead, he said, their concern should be with setting up *batei midrash*, with helping poor people earn money and with helping everyone to learn Torah.

In this way did the Maharal take charge of the rabbinate in Posen.

In the meantime, the Maharal's family was growing. The Maharal and his wife gained a great-grandchild, a girl born to Shmuel, son of Betzalel. And not long after this, another girl was born to Shmuel.

Besides his public occupations as rabbi of Posen and all of Poland, the Maharal continued his Torah writing, and in 1595, he published his *Nesivos Olam*. In some ways a continuation of *Derech Hachaim*, *Nesivos Olam* deals with the previously-introduced material in a more detailed and specific manner.

24

On the Road Again

"MAMA, MAMA!"

Perl rose up and walked across the room to greet her daughter Feigeleh. On Perl's face, happiness at seeing her daughter was mixed with sadness.

"My dear daughter," Perl exclaimed, squeezing her daughter's hands in hers, "you shouldn't have come all the way from Prague!"

"But I had to see you! Where is Father?"

"He is in the *beis midrash*. He'll be back at dinner-time."

"Oh, mama! I was so upset to hear!"

"*Baruch Dayan Emes*," said Perl serenely, though her eyes glinted with tears. "Your Uncle Yitzchak lived a good, long life. I'm happy for that."

"Oh, mama, you must be so sad, so very sad. The news got to you . . . ?"

"Just last week. Your father kept it from me so I wouldn't have to sit *shiva*."

Her daughter looked at her with deep compassion, and Perl squeezed her hands again. "Come, my dear, you must be tired after the journey. Let's sit down, and I'll get you something to eat."

She led her daughter into the kitchen, and soon they were sitting at the table, eating cake and drinking tea.

"Do you think that now Father might come back to Prague and accept the position of Chief Rabbi?" Feigeleh asked.

"Your father has been talking of going back to Prague," Perl said. "But of course, Rabbi Yaffe is leading the community now."

"Yes, that's so," answered Feigeleh. "But there are rumors that he might be leaving."

"Rumors are just rumors," Perl said. "In my lifetime, I have heard many rumors."

"But we were thinking," persisted Feigeleh. "When Uncle Yitzchak was alive, Father might not have wanted to be Chief Rabbi because it might have hurt Uncle Yitzchak's feelings, after he had to step down. But now, people are saying . . ."

"My dear, people may be saying, but your father isn't saying anything. He only says that he is considering moving back to Prague. But nothing more than that."

"It must be hard for you, mama."

"Hashem has blessed me with a great Torah scholar for a husband, wonderful children and grandchildren," said Perl. "Drink your tea, Feigeleh, before it grows cold."

When the Maharal came home in the evening, he greeted his daughter with warm affection.

At the dinner table, he announced, "I've made up my mind. I intend to resign my position here and move back to Prague."

"And Posen . . . ?" Perl said.

THE MAHARAL

"It is possible that Rabbi Yaffe will be interested in taking over my position, and the community leaders have said they would accept him."

"So you will be Chief Rabbi of Prague, finally!" exclaimed Feigeleh.

But the Maharal said nothing.

"Tzaddik ba la'ir! A *tzaddik* has come to the city!"

Months had passed. Now the Maharal was making a triumphant return to Prague. Government representatives, community leaders, Talmudic sages and Rabbi Yaffe, the Chief Rabbi himself, all welcomed him at a festive public ceremony where the masses jostled against each other to catch a glimpse of the holy *tzaddik*. Mothers raised their toddlers high in the air to see him and be blessed, young boys gazed at him and dreamed of one day becoming as great as he, young girls looked at him and dreamed of catching a husband with such nobility and holiness.

The Maharal returned to his old home and *beis midrash*, and his many children, in-laws and grandchildren crowded about his table on *Shabbos* and rejoiced in his return.

Weeks passed by, and Posen formally offered the post of Chief Rabbi to Rabbi Yaffe.

Rabbi Yaffe accepted the offer and returned to Posen, the city he had left five years earlier, when the Maharal had left Prague. He was sent off with great honor and love. But the people were not bereft, for the Maharal was among them.

Shortly afterwards, Mordechai Meisel, who rejoiced to bask again in the light of his master's face, reported to the Maharal, "The community leaders are going to ask you to accept the post of Chief Rabbi."

"I will accept," the Maharal replied.

And so at last, when the Maharal was already in his late eighties, at an age when most people have completed their

THE MAHARAL

life's work, he became Chief Rabbi of Prague, leader of the city to whose name he was to be forever linked.

In his youth, the Maharal had been such a brilliant student, such a prodigy and so wise that it had been predicted that he would have an early, brilliant career as rabbi.

But the Maharal had disappointed those about him. While other young men were become rabbis and receiving rabbinical posts, the Maharal remained in the *beis midrash*. Although acknowledged as a Torah leader, he neither led a community nor authored *sefarim*.

Like a large vessel that fills slowly, the Maharal spent the decades of his youth and middle age preparing himself for the work that lay ahead.

From precociousness, the Maharal had patiently moved to maturity and depth. A young genius may flash brilliantly like lightning. But the Maharal's wisdom glowed brightly and steadily. His community activity was a solid accomplishment measured in the improvement of life for tens of thousands of Jews; his educational reforms were taking hold, and would eventually help change the face of Torah learning in Central and Eastern Europe for centuries to come; his Torah writings would come to inspire great Torah leaders and thinkers, down to the present day, who used his writings to revitalize the commitment to Torah among their followers.

Maharal, Chief Rabbi of Prague! It was not the title that enhanced the man, but the man who gave meaning to the title.

Perl's pride in the accomplishments of her husband were boundless. He had attained greatness in all areas of his life, and she stood at his side. She supported him and was with him in every step of his life. The years with him had been good years.

25

Thaddeus and the Golem

THE CONSTANT RETELLING OF THIS STORY OF THE MAHARAL'S PHE-
nomenal powers makes it hard to ignore, although no one is sure of its authenticity. According to the popular tale, as told in *Niflaos Hamaharal* by Rabbi Yudel Rosenberg (Pietrkov 1909), the story was as follows:

Dr. Marizi poured himself a full glass of purple wine and slung it down with a smooth and practiced bobbing of his adam's apple.

"Pah!" he exclaimed, setting the glass down heavily. "Who makes these awful Passover wines? You could get sick as a mad dog!" He shivered. "Good thing I'm a doctor, and I can heal the bite with the dog's tail." His words were slurred, and it was clear that he had been involved in this mode of self-medication for some time. He poured himself another glass from a bottle made of cut glass that glinted in the sunlight, and sipped it appreciatively. "Real claret! Now that's a blessed change." Suddenly, he dashed the half-full cup onto the table, and the wine spilled across the tablecloth like a crushed flower.

"But dash it, what's going to happen to Sophia?" He put his head in his hands and gave a sob. Then he jerked his head up. "That isn't going to solve anything."

He got up and walked heavily up and down the room. "I may not be a good Jew, but at least I'm a *Jew*!" With this last word, he swept his hand out and knocked down the bottle of sweet wine. "And when Rivkah died, I thought that I would at least raise Sophia to be some kind of a good daughter, and a Jew!"

As he lumbered past the table, he sent one of the wine glasses flying against the wall, where it smashed into a thousand splinters to the floor.

"And now, that little vixen has gone off to become a Christian and she's left me all alone!" His voice rose in anger and self-pity, and he beat his fist on the table. "And she's only fifteen! My baby!" Marizi sank onto a chair, buried his face in his hands and broke out into desperate, dry sobs.

Meanwhile, Sophia Marizi was hungrily eating a chicken leg and looking at the priest who was taking such a kind interest in her. The priest was called Father Thaddeus.

"Eat your chicken, dear," he murmured, his gleaming eyes fixed on hers. "Have all you want. We have plenty here."

"Thank you, Father Thaddeus. But what's going to happen next?"

"Well, my dear," murmured Father Thaddeus, "next, you will take the step of saving your soul from the eternal flames of damnation."

Sophia's eyes opened wide, and she ceased to chew on her chicken.

THE MAHARAL

Thaddeus's voice grew sad and piteous. "Think of all the poor souls who must burn forever!"

Sophia's voice was a bare whisper. "Why, Father Thaddeus?"

"Why?" Father Thaddeus roared. "Because they haven't been saved! Because their damnable parents, stiff-necked, obstinate sinners did not baptize them in our religion. We told them, too. We offered them wealth and success if they would be baptized—and they refused." He paused. "Eat, my child."

Sophia swallowed hard. "I can't."

"No, how can anyone eat when he contemplates that the Jews will always be condemned?"

"Oh!" Sophia burst into a sob.

"Ah, but you," Thaddeus said gently, "you shall be saved. You shall save your soul, and instead of hellfire, you shall inherit eternal bliss in the presence of the saints, where the celestial choirs play a music so sweet that it thrills the soul to ever-greater ecstasy."

"And I'll have friends?" Sophia asked.

"Friends?" replied Thaddeus. "The saints shall be your companions, and the cherubs your playmates."

"Oh, it sounds so beautiful!" said Sophia, and she bit into her chicken again.

"Oh, it is, it is," agreed Thaddeus. "Very beautiful." His eyes gleamed strangely as he stared hard at Sophia, who was again busy chewing. "Of course, you must prove deserving of being baptized."

"Sure," said Sophia.

Thaddeus laughed. "Yes, of course. Sure. I know how worthy you will prove yourself. Listen! Sophia looked up in alarm, putting down the chicken leg. "Will you say whatever I tell you, even if it does not seem true, in order to save your soul?"

Sophia nodded dumbly.

"Speak!" roared Thaddeus. "Are you prepared to renounce evil and embrace goodness?"

"Yes!" said Sophia.

"Will you do whatever you must do for the sake of saving your soul?"

"Yes," said Sophia in a small, frightened voice.

"And when you save your soul, you will ease the torment of your dear, departed mother who even now is burning and screaming in the eternal flames of hell! Do you want to help her, or do you want to let her burn?"

Sophia started crying again. "I want to help her!"

Thaddeus's voice grew soft again. "Of course you do, child. Sweet child." Sophia sobbed, and Thaddeus spoke gently. "Listen to me. This is what you must do. Tomorrow the cardinal will come and question you before you can be baptized. This is what I want you to tell him.

"Tell him that you are becoming a Christian because you can no longer endure the cruelty of the Jews. Tell him that right before Passover, the two servants of that interfering, troublesome rabbi of the Jews, Rabbi Loew, came to your father late at night and you overheard their conversation. Say that you saw them give your father a bottle of blood, which they brought for him to mix with the dough when he makes his Jewish *matzah*. Say that you saw your father pay the servants a great deal of money for the blood. Do you understand that?"

"But—it's not true, and it's disgusting, and they would never do such an awful thing!"

"Do you want to burn?" Thaddeus screamed.

Some sixth sense told her that the kind Father Thaddeus meant that threat seriously, and the frightened girl nodded her head.

"Good, very good. Now, one more thing, child. Tell the cardinal that you heard one of the servants say that the blood

THE MAHARAL

was taken from Lucrezia, the servant girl—"

"But my father says she ran away to her home!"

"Do you wish to burn forever?" roared Thaddeus.

"No," said Sophia in a meek voice.

"Tell the priest exactly as I have told you, and you will be baptized, and I will take you to a convent where you shall find all the friends you want, and the most lovely, joyful life you could imagine, with cake, chicken, new clothes and friends every day!"

"Every day?"

"I promise you, Sophia!"

The next day, Sophia spoke to the cardinal exactly as Father Thaddeus had counseled her.

"Are you quite sure of what you are telling me?" the cardinal said, when she had finished stumbling through her tale.

"Oh yes, I really am. I am saying exactly what I should say. I am sure I haven't forgotten anything!" said Sophia. "Now will you baptize me, please?"

The cardinal baptized Sophia, though in his heart he harbored doubts about the story she had told. She seemed so young, so gullible, so frightened. And Thaddeus seemed a little too closely interested in her. Could it be that Thaddeus had somehow engineered this? No, he mustn't entertain questions about a fellow priest! Yet her story seemed so mechanical, and she had spilled out the words as though she had rehearsed them. Where did the truth lie?

The cardinal returned to his study and there, with some hesitation, wrote up a report of the strange tale that the girl had reported, one copy of which he sent to the court and another to the Maharal.

When the Maharal received this account, he trembled. When would this most bitter exile end? How long must the Jews, the chosen people of Hashem, be quarry of the most degraded creatures, animals in human form, who out of spite or mere sport had the freedom to oppress, to starve, to torment and kill the Jews, as a brutal boy might wantonly torment a defenseless butterfly whose brilliant wings made beautiful the pastureland?

The Maharal knew that his two servants would be seized by the government and jailed. One of his servants was his trusty man, Avraham Chaim. But the other servant was the tall and massive servant, the mute and expressionless Yossele. Only the Maharal and a few close confidantes knew that Yossele was in reality a *golem*, a figure formed of clay and imbued with life by the Maharal's great powers of Kabbalah, a figure whom the Maharal employed to protect the Jews precisely from such evil schemes.

The Maharal devised a plan to keep the *golem* free. "Go quickly, before you are yourself arrested," he told the unhappy Avraham Chaim. "Seek out in the marketplace, amidst the teeming throng, a deaf-mute who resembles, even slightly, Yossele the *golem*."

"Do you mean to have him switch places with Yossele?" asked Avraham.

"Yes, Avraham. We can only hope that this girl, Sophia, will be misled to mistake the one for the other. And in the meantime, the *golem* will be free to help resolve this tragic farce."

Avraham did as the Maharal instructed him. He roused the *golem* from his place, made him change his clothes and took him to another house to stay. Avraham then went to the marketplace, where he found an indigent deaf-mute, a large, lumbering man, and invited him to supper. The man was fed a large dinner and plied with great amounts of liquor. Gratefully, the old hobo ate and drank as much as he could, and then, as he began to sag onto the table, Avraham helped him up. He walked him over to Yossele's bed, onto which the deaf-

THE MAHARAL

mute fell heavily and began snoring. Avraham pulled the man's clothes off and put Yossele's clothing on the chair next to the bed.

That midnight, soldiers surrounded the house of the Maharal and banged on his door.

"What is it?" cried the Maharal.

"Open up in the name of the law," the sergeant called out. "We're here to arrest your servant Yossele on a charge of selling the blood of a Christian martyr!"

The Maharal allowed the soldiers into the house and showed them the room where the *golem* stayed. The soldiers roused the still-drunken old beggar who, not noticing that his clothes had been switched, hazily put on the clothes of the *golem* and stumbled out into the cold night air surrounded by the soldiers.

Meanwhile, a similar raid had been made on the house of Avraham Chaim.

The next morning, both men were arraigned before the court, charges formally leveled at them, and a court date was set four weeks from that day.

Fear and consternation spread throughout the Prague ghetto. The Maharal himself was in danger of being arrested—already, he had been summoned as a material witness—and the Jews repaired to the synagogues to wail and pray before Hashem to save them.

The Maharal, in the meantime, walked back and forth in his study, thinking with furious concentration. "It seems to me that the weak link in this matter is Lucrezia," he mused, "the missing servantgirl who, the prosecution alleges, was murdered. If I could only find some hint, some sort of clue." The Maharal went to the door and called out, "Shimshon!"

A moment later, a red-headed, freckled young man hurried to the Maharal's study. "Yes, Rabbi Loew?"

"Now listen, Shimshon. This is what I want you to do. Go

THE MAHARAL

to the people that Lucrezia was working for. Speak to them and find out what they know about her disappearance. And I also want you to get as exact a description of her as you can. Here." The Maharal reached into a drawer and pulled out five gold pieces. "This may help loosen their tongues. As soon as you get the information, hurry right back here and report. I'll be waiting for you."

"Yes, Rabbi Loew."

Shimshon pocketed the gold pieces and hurried from the study. All that afternoon, the Maharal waited anxiously. "There's nothing to be gained by worrying," he told himself, and he sat down at his desk to study from a volume of the Talmud.

Finally, Shimshon came back, his face beaming.

The Maharal placed a gold strip that he used as a bookmark into his *sefer*, and put it down on his desk. "You've got something," he said.

"Yes, Rabbi," replied Shimshon. "Shall I report in full, or do you just want to hear the essentials?"

"The essentials will do," the Maharal said.

"I talked with the girl's employer, Friedrich Pletzl. He didn't want to talk at first, but I smoothed him over with the gold coins. He said that Lucrezia had been unhappy with the way that they were treating her, and that she had started threatening to run away and go home."

"Excellent," said the Maharal. "Where does she live?"

"That part's tricky," said Shimshon. "Her boss had heard her mention the names of several villages and farms, but he didn't remember which was hers. I eventually talked to his wife and man-servant. They didn't know exactly where Lucrezia came from, but I narrowed it down to two villages and two farms."

Shimshon told the names of the four places to the Maharal, who wrote them down on a sheet of paper.

THE MAHARAL

"I have some more work for you," said the Maharal. "But I'll need three more operatives. Go to the *beis midrash* and call Shaul, Volf and Baruch Ber."

Soon the three young men, together with Shimshon, were assembled in the Maharal's study.

The Maharal explained the situation to them succinctly. "Now each of you is to go to one of these places and look for Lucrezia. Shimshon, you describe her and give each man twenty gold coins from my cash box. That should be enough to cover your travelling expenses and whatever you may need for bribes. I don't have to tell you that time is of the essence. Start out today and return as soon as you can!"

The four young men hired carriages and rode out of Prague to the four locations.

After twelve days passed, the four at last returned.

Again, they met in the Maharal's study. The Maharal was bitterly disappointed to hear their reports. Each of the men stated that no one had admitted to knowing anything of Lucrezia's whereabouts. If Lucrezia was in one of those locations, she didn't want to be found.

The Maharal dismissed the three students and told Shimshon, "Go to the house of Reb Chanina, and tell him to bring you in to Yossele."

"But Yossele is in jail!"

"Things will be made clearer to you later. Right now, when you come to Yossele, tell him that I told him to go with you, and bring him right back here to me."

As Shimshon left, the Maharal sat down at his desk and began composing a letter.

Dear Lucrezia,

Maria and I are so very sorry that you have left us. We understand why you did so, and we want to say that we are sorry for having mistreated you. We realize that it was wrong to beat you with the teakettle for consorting with Ivan the bootblack.

We want you to know that we are prepared to raise your salary and allow you to marry Ivan.

Both Maria and I miss you very much, and Ivan is crying every day because you are gone. Please hurry back. The man who hands you this letter is very reliable. He will bring you back to us, who miss you very much.

Dimitri

Not half an hour later, Yossele the *golem* stood before, the Maharal. The *golem* stood unblinking and motionless, his large, hammy hands hanging down straight from his shoulders.

"Listen, Yossele," said the Maharal. "Here is a list of two villages and two farms. You are to go to each of them and search for the servant girl named Lucrezia, who is in hiding. Do you know her?"

The *golem* nodded.

"Good. When you find her, give her this letter. Here are ten gold coins for your expenses."

The *golem* silently put out his huge hand and took the letter and money that the Maharal handed him.

Two weeks passed, and there was no sign of Yossele. The Maharal was heart-broken. The day before the trial was to begin, he declared a general fast and announced that on the day of the court proceedings, all the Jews of Prague should spend the day in the synagogue, praying and saying *Tehillim*.

The courtroom was thronged with onlookers, both Jewish and Christian. First arrived the judges, then Thaddeus and Sophia, and then the Maharal. Finally, Avraham Chaim and the deaf-mute were brought in wearing chains. When the Maharal saw this sad sight, tears sprung to his eyes.

THE MAHARAL

First, Avraham Chaim was questioned about the girl's story, and he forcefully denied any knowledge of her accusations.

After him, the deaf-mute was put on the stand. The judge lifted up a small vessel filled with a red liquid and asked the deaf-mute if he had ever carried such things, simultaneously motioning with his hands.

The deaf-mute nodded brightly, a smile on his face. He put his thumb to his mouth and made a dumb-show of drinking.

"He seems to think I'm offering him some wine to drink," the judge commented.

"Point of order! Point of order!" cried Thaddeus. He leaped up from his seat and addressed the judge. "As your honor may observe, this deaf-mute is rather trying to tell us that the Jews drank the blood."

The defending counsel now arose. "I shall now question the witness whether he is aware of any truth to the charge that the Maharal had the servant-girl killed and collected her blood in a bottle." He pulled a knife from his clothing and held the naked blade against his throat. Then he pointed at the Maharal and at the bottle of red liquid.

The deaf-mute excitedly shook his head from side to side.

"It seems that the witness denies any such allegation," observed the judge.

"Point of order! Point of order!" Thaddeus again jumped up from his seat. "I object to the interpretation of the witness's testimony."

"I object, your honor!" called out the defense attorney. "Father Thaddeus clearly lacks expertise."

"Please, stop this squabbling," the judge interrupted, ringing his bell in irritation. "This is a trial, not an educational institute for understanding the deaf. If the witness cannot be understood, let him step down. Have the plaintiff, Sophia, called to the stand."

Sophia then stepped up to the stand and stuck by her original testimony, claiming to recognize Avraham Chaim and the deaf-mute as the two servants who had brought her father a bottle of blood.

The defense counsel stood up. "I request that Dr. Marizi be summoned to give testimony."

The judge looked down at him. "He has been summoned, but he cannot be located."

"In that case," replied the defense counsel. "I hereby move that—"

Suddenly, there was a commotion at the back door of the court. Amidst a great deal of shouting and a wild tumult, Yossele burst into the courtroom, one broad and tawny arm wrapped about Lucrezia, the missing servant-girl.

Thaddeus and Sophia stared, horror-stricken, to see Lucrezia looking so very much alive and—literally—kicking. They knew that their case had just been demolished.

Lucrezia was brought up to the stand. She apologized for her uncivilized entrance, saying that Yossele had first gone to the Maharal's house and, seeing it empty, had hurried at a breakneck pace to the courtyard. She testified that she had never been molested by Jews, nor her blood used in any ceremony, and added that if anything of this nature had occurred, she would have been the first to know about it.

The court now called up the Maharal to speak. To the general astonishment and admiration of the assembly, the Maharal described how he had deduced that Lucrezia was the missing link to the case and how, with the help of his servant Yossele he had located her.

The judge commended the Maharal and invited him to sit at his side, where he warmly shook the rabbi's hand.

Thaddeus, although marked with disgrace, had been clever enough to keep his guilt unprovable and the court was forced to let him free, although Sophia screamed and blamed him for his perfidy. Sophia herself was sentenced to six years' imprisonment for providing false testimony, and she was led away in shock and tears.

And the Jews laughed and wept at this sudden miracle, and thanked Heaven for the great gift that they had been given—the extraordinary person of the Maharal.

26

Blossoming Thoughts

IN THE NEXT FEW YEARS, THE MAHARAL WORKED STEADILY ON HIS writing.

He had conceived the idea, as noted in the introduction to *Gur Aryeh*, to write a six-volume series that would present his understanding of the Torah's world-view, tied to a presentation of *Shabbos* and each of the Jewish holidays. The titles of the volumes were to be connected to the verse said in the morning prayers, "To You, Hashem, are the greatness and the power and the beauty, and the eternity and the glory, for everything in the heavens and in the earth [is Yours]." (*Divrei Hayamim I* 29:11)

The series would encompass the following volumes: *Sefer Hagedulah* (*The Book of Greatness*) on *Shabbos*; *Sefer Hagevurah* (*The Book of Power*) on *Pesach*; *Sefer Hatiferes* (*The Book of Beauty*) on *Shavuos*; *Sefer Netzach* (*The Book of Eternity*) on *Tishah b'Av* and *Mashiach*; *Sefer Hod* (*The Book of Glory*) on *Sukkos*; *Sefer Shamayim Vaaretz* (*The Book of Heaven and Earth*) on *Rosh Hashanah* and *Yom Kippur*.

Sefer Hagevurah had already been printed under the name of *Gevuros Hashem*. Besides this, the Maharal only printed two other works of this series: *Tiferes Yisrael* (that is, *Sefer Hatiferes*) and *Netzach Yisrael* (*Sefer Netzach*). It is not known whether he did not manage to complete the series, or whether the manuscripts were lost or destroyed in the fire of 1689, which burned a number of his writings.

Between 1598 and 1600, the Maharal completed and printed five more *sefarim*.

The first volume was *Tiferes Yisrael*. This *sefer* discusses such topics as the giving of the Torah, the importance of serving Hashem through learning Torah and doing *mitzvos* rather than through philosophical insight, and the truth of the written and the oral Torah. The *sefer* also discusses related matters such as Hebrew pronunciation and comes to the conclusion that the Ashkenazi dialect is the correct pronunciation.

The second volume was *Be'er Hagolah* (which had actually been written many years earlier). This work justifies the truth and wisdom of the Talmud, and in particular deals with many apparently strange *Midrashim*, explaining their inherent wisdom and truth.

The Maharal took the opportunity in *Be'er Hagolah* to sharply criticize *Meor Einayim*, a work which had appeared in 1573-1575, as well as other statements by Azaria de Rossi (1511-1578) of Italy. Rossi, although an observant Jew, employed an approach to the Talmud that seemed to be no different from the approach one would employ when studying a secular work. A rationalist, Rossi came to many conclusions that tended to disparage the quality of the Talmud. It was only natural that, in defending the value and legitimacy of the oral Torah, the Maharal should deal with the *Meor Einayim*, which misled people because of its obvious scholarship.

The third volume, *Netzach Yisrael*, deals with the destruction of the *Beis Hamikdash* and the restoration of the Jewish nation with the coming of *Mashiach*.

The fourth volume was *Ohr Chadash*, which deals with the holiday of *Purim*, explaining both the Book of Esther and various statements in *Megillah*.

The fifth volume is *Ner Mitzvah*, dealing with the deeper meaning of *Chanukah*.

In addition, the Maharal produced a number of *halachic* volumes.

One particularly intriguing work was unfortunately destroyed in the fire of 1689. This was a reconstruction of the *Gemara* on the *Mishnaic* orders of *Zeraim* and *Taharos*, based on statements scattered throughout the Talmud, with three accompanying commentaries: the first in the style of Rashi; the second in the style of the Rif; and the third in the style of the *Tosafos*.

One other volume attributed by some to the Maharal is *Piskei Bitchonos*, a collection of verses whose purpose is to nullify evil decrees. This is said to have originally been the work of the Maharal's great-grandfather, the famous Kabbalist whose name was also Rabbi Yehudah Loew.

The Maharal employed a singular writing style. At times, the Maharal would create a new word, based on an established root, to present an idea. Although in a number of places, the Maharal demonstrated his clear knowledge of Hebrew grammar, he sometimes invented new, ungrammatical constructions to give expression to his original concepts.

The Maharal commented, "If something is understandable, one does not have to be too careful about the grammar." (*Nesivos Olam*)

THE MAHARAL

"Poetry and songs are not written in a language that is so easily understood. This is because poems emerge from joy and a good heart...Whatever is connected to joy speaks of distant matters. When the heart of the composer is open, he speaks in hyperbole. All song contains exaggeration. Since in its essence it is not like normal speech, its language is not entirely in accord with grammar." (*Nesivos Olam*)

"This is song: desire of the created being for its Creator." (*Gevuros Hashem*)

The Maharal had hundreds of students, many of whom became great teachers in their own right.

Rabbi David Gans was the author of *Tzemach David*, an important historical work. Interested in all branches of wisdom, he was friendly with the great astronomer Tycho Brahe (1546-1601), who lived close to Prague from 1598-1609, where he served as astrologer to King Rudolf. Rabbi Gans visited his observatory three times, where he was deeply impressed with Brahe's work, exclaiming, "I will truly say that we never saw or heard such great investigations in all our days, nor did our fathers tell us of such things, nor have we found such matters written in any book—neither from Jews nor, *lehavdil*, from the nations of the world."

Rabbi Gans also met the astronomers Johann Kepler and Johann Miller at the court of King Rudolf.

Legend also tells that King Rudolf and Tycho Brahe once paid a visit to the Maharal. In order to host his guests properly, the Maharal brought the entire Hradschin Castle (the old royal castle of Prague) into his house. King Rudolf was so amazed at this extraordinary feat that he showered the Maharal with great wealth and honors.

Another student of the Maharal was Rabbi Yom Tov Heller (1579-1654). Rabbi Yom Tov Heller, greatly influenced by the Maharal's great predilection for learning *Mishnah*, authored the famous commentary *Tosafos Yom Tov*. Also like the

THE MAHARAL

Maharal, he had a special love for the commentary of the Rosh, and he wrote his own commentary on *Piskei Harosh*, using the Rosh's *halachic* decisions as a model of how to interpret and decide *halachah*. Rabbi Heller was also involved in learning Kabbalah and philosophy and was well-acquainted with the sciences of his day, including mathematics, geography and astronomy, which he made use of in *Tosafos Yom Tov*.

Again like the Maharal, Rabbi Heller served as a chief rabbi—and, in Vienna, he too produced a series of *takanos*, including a renewal of the Maharal's *takanah* of a *mi shebeirach* for those who do not speak during prayers.

A third student of the Maharal was Rabbi Eliyahu Loanz of Worms (1564–1636). Rabbi Loanz, grandson of Rabbi Yosef Joselmann, famous *shtadlan* (activist) of Rosheim, was chief rabbi in various localities, principally Worms. He was well-known as a Kabbalist and miracle-worker who wrote *kamayos* (amulets) and he was as a result known as Eliyahu Baal Shem (Master of [God's] Name).

Rabbi Eliyahu wrote a number of Kabbalistic works, such as *Rinas Dodim* on *Shir Hashirim* and *Aderess Eliyahu*, a commentary on the *Zohar*. He also wrote commentaries on *Koheles* and *Chovos Halevavos*. He prepared a number of *halachic* works for publication, among them the Rema's *Darkei Moshe*.

He also wrote poetry, including the secular poem, *Vikuach Yayin im Mayim*, which was translated into German. In addition, he carried out a correspondence with the gentile Hebraist, Johannes Buxtorf.

The Maharal also had a lasting influence on the famous *darshan* Rabbi Shlomo Ephraim of Luntschitz. For instance, the influence of the Maharal's approach to Torah learning can be clearly seen in Rabbi Luntschitz's sermon, recorded in *Amudei Sheish*: "All the teaching in the *yeshivah* comes down to the empty arguments of *chilluk*. It is terrible to think that some elderly rabbi teaches this, even though he and everyone else know that the true meaning is different. Can Hashem really want that we should sharpen our minds with such false teachings?. . .This type of study [of *chilluk–pilpul*] has an especially negative effect on the students. There might be a student who, if he had been able to learn *Tanach*, *Mishnah*, Talmud and *Halachah* in a regular, orderly fashion, would have shone as one of the best. But if this student does not excel in empty *chilluk*, he is looked down upon to the point that he is practically forced to stop learning. I myself have known intelligent young men who, when they couldn't shine in *pilpul*, were considered inept by their fellow-students and so gave up learning altogether upon getting married."

One of the first things the Maharal did upon returning from Posen to Prague was to help Rabbi Yosef Heilperin of Posen publish *Eim Hayeled*, a Hebrew grammar for seven-year-old children. In his preface, Rabbi Heilperin wrote that the Maharal had urged him to produce this work, and the Maharal himself added a line that one is obligated to teach one's children the Holy Tongue in a clear manner, just as was done in previous generations.

In the meantime, the Maharal continued his campaign for the learning of *Mishnah* by both children and adults, those who knew little and those who were learned.

The Maharal wanted that adults and learned people learn *Mishnah*, and thus he established *Chevros Mishnayos* that learned one chapter of *Mishnah* a day. In this way, one could go through the entire six orders of the *Mishnah* in a few years and gain a comprehension of and familiarity with the basic concepts discussed in the entire Talmud. The first such group was organized in Prague, but gradually this institution spread across all of Europe. The Maharal wished that the *Mishnah* be learned with comprehension. As his student Rabbi Yom Tov Heller wrote, the intent was "to teach *Mishnah* with attention to its reasons and commentaries."

27

The Elder Years

RABBI BETZALEL, SON OF THE MAHARAL, REJOICED IN HIS HEART, FOR his daughter Shlift was to be married and her husband-to-be was a jewel. Rabbi Pinchas Halevi Horowitz, who began his career as Chief Rabbi of Ploda and later became a judge in Prague, was known as an important *Halachic* authority and Kabbalist.

But Rabbi Betzalel and his wife suffered great heartbreak as well, for their son Menachem, a brilliant young man who had been noted for his expertise in the *Turim*, passed away.

In those times, the Maharal's hair was snowy-white, and he was no longer as tall as he had been. One day, as he came to the *beis midrash*, he fell into a faint. When he awoke, he was lying on a bench with the doctor bending over him.

"Don't talk, please," the doctor was saying. "I'll be making a hot drink for you. Can you drink? Just nod your head."

THE MAHARAL

The Maharal weakly nodded his head. "Doctor, I—"

"Please don't talk, Rabbi Loew. You aren't well, and you have to rest. Do you understand me?"

The Maharal nodded again, and the doctor's face receded into the blurry background.

A few moments later, someone took the Maharal's pale, wrinkled hand in his. The Maharal looked up at Betzalel.

"Father, Father, you'll be all right!"

The Maharal made as if to speak. "Father! The doctor said not to talk. You need to rest."

Betzalel sat next to his father, holding his hand and gazing into his eyes, and the Maharal felt comforted.

He was half-asleep and hardly aware when he was placed upon a stretcher and carried out of the *beis midrash* and brought to his bed at home. He slept fitfully, and whenever he awoke, he saw Perl's anxious face.

In the morning, he felt better, and he had a thin soup with noodles.

There was a flow of visitors, family and friends, but his wife saw how tired he was and no longer let them visit. Thus did he lie in bed, and over the course of the next few weeks, he slowly recuperated, until he felt strong enough to get up from his bed and even to walk about the apartment.

By the end of the month, the Maharal was out of the house and again going to the *beis midrash* to learn. He was again dealing with the volume of mail that came to him and answering the pressing questions that he had to attend to as chief rabbi.

One day, Mordechai Meisel, who was also aging, was interrupted in his room by his servant, who told him, "Rabbi Loew is here to see you, sir."

Mordechai Meisel hurried to the parlor and invited the Maharal in. "Rabbi Loew," he said, "you should never have come here. You merely had to call on me and I would have

THE MAHARAL

been delighted to go to you, you know that."

As Meisel talked volubly, they made their way to Meisel's study.

"I have come to you because I can no longer discharge all of my duties," the Maharal said. "My son Betzalel is a very learned man—I know that people call him Betzalel *Charif*, Betzalel the Sharp—and I want him to take over as head of the *yeshivah*. But I know how bitterly the community leaders fight over every appointment, and I know that there are some leaders who still oppose me."

"You can be assured that I will do everything I can to see that your son becomes head of the *yeshivah*," Meisel assured the Maharal. "I will go myself and speak with some of the board members."

"Thank you, Reb Meisel."

That afternoon, Mordechai Meisel paid a visit to Reb Meir, an important member of the community board.

When Reb Meir heard Meisel's request that he approve Rabbi Betzalel as head of the *yeshivah*, he shook his head doubtfully and pursed his lips.

"This hardly seems regular," he said, looking up at Meisel through narrowed eyes. "This is becoming quite a family affair."

"What do you mean?"

"Why, you know that there are people on the board who for years—have been complaining that Rabbi Loew has altogether too much power. I mean, I disagree with them, of course. He's a grand old man and a really great rabbi. But I mean, they have a point, in a way, you know." He stopped to take out a silver box and take a pinch of snuff.

"My dear Meisel, it is only common sense that when some of the board members hear that he wants to make his own son head of the *yeshivah*, they'll be absolutely *furious*. Not that I agree with them, of course, but after all, they have a point.

THE MAHARAL

I tell you, Meisel, I've always done as much as I can for Rabbi Loew, but you know, I cannot go too far. If I stuck my neck out for you on this one, I'd only lose my seat, and where would we be then?"

"Then you're saying that you won't help Rabbi Loew."

"I'm not saying *that*, my friend. I'll help him all I can. You know how much I value Rabbi Loew. But I can't do the *impossible*, you must see the justice in *that*."

Furious, Meisel went to another community board member, Reb Elchanan.

"I'll do what I can," Reb Elchanan promised. "But I'm doubtful that it will do much good."

"Why not?"

"Look around you. Just look at the number of influential people in the community who have gotten even more powerful by appointing their children or relatives to important posts. How about Naftali, for instance? After his son became a wheat dealer, he pushed through a law that wheat from out of Prague can't be used because it might contain worms. Of course, that just happened to mean that his son got all the business and grew very rich. Or how about Nachum Weiss, who made a building code that all buildings have to be built of a certain type of wood, which his brother-in-law just happens to deal in?"

"Are you telling me that you think that the Maharal would appoint his son so that he could—"

"No, I don't think anything of the kind. But I can assure you that that's what the other community board members will think. Don't be naive! If you weren't so eager to help the Maharal—and who could blame you?—you'd see it yourself! You know that when small-minded men look upon a great man, all they see is a reflection of themselves. These community board members know that they have power and the Maharal has power. They know how they got power and how they would like to get more power, and they assume that the Maharal is just like them, except that he's chief rabbi while they're community board members."

"Yes," said Meisel. "Just as the gentiles look at the Jews, and think the worst of us. Still, I'm not going to give up without a fight."

"And I'm on your side. But I'm warning you, it won't be easy."

The appointment proposal was brought to the community board at its next meeting. As Naftali had predicted, the fight for the appointment of Betzalel as head of the *yeshivah* was far from certain. Meisel was astounded at how many board members dared to challenge the Maharal.

"No one honors, respects and values Rabbi Loew more than I," declaimed one speaker. "No one can match my gratitude and my complete devotion to Rabbi Loew, a complete *tzaddik*, a holy man who is completely enveloped in the spirit of the Torah. And so in this spirit of awe, in this awareness of the greatness of Rabbi Loew, beyond all distinction that I myself could attain or conceive of, I must be honest—yes, friends, I must be honest, no matter how much that might hurt! no matter how much that might offend and disturb!—and I must courageously state that a leader of such a caliber sometimes lacks awareness of the banalities of day-to-day decision making. The Maharal's greatness is in Torah. But we community board members have been given the responsibility for day-to-day life in Prague, for that is our prerogative. Thus it has been and thus must we view it as the will of Hashem Himself. No one can possibly conceive a greater regard for Rabbi Loew than I—"

The speeches were interminable, and Meisel worked frantically with a few other supporters to secure support for Rabbi Betzalel. What a disgrace it would be if the community of Prague was to reject the Maharal's recommendation for head of the *yeshivah*! It would be a slap in the face to the Maharal and to his son, and it would be a mark of shame for Prague. Certainly, the community board members could not allow such a thing to occur.

At last the vote was taken, and the members' voices rang out, one after the other, "Aye! Nay! Nay! Nay!" Meisel himself called out in a strong voice, "Aye!" and he was gratified that several board members who had originally been undecided voted in favor of Rabbi Betzalel. Nervously, he jotted down the number of Ayes and Nays. When the vote was over, Meisel was shattered. The community board had voted against the appointment of Rabbi Betzalel.

When the Maharal heard the result of the vote later that day, he was deeply saddened. He gazed out his window at the verdant hills beyond the city. It was not personal feelings, and it was not bitterness, for he knew from long experience how small-minded people could be, and that it was a great error to take that small-mindedness personally—for to the contrary, it was precisely against those greater than themselves that small-minded people displayed the greatest animus.

But still, it was a blow—not only to him, his wife Perl and his son Betzalel but also to the Maharal's hopes that after so many decades of effort, he would be able to put an end to the destructive backbiting and controversy among the community board members of Prague. This was not only a plague of itself, but it betrayed a lack of love among Jews and a lack of unity that could only extend the bitter exile.

The community board instead appointed Rabbi Shlomo Ephraim of Luntschitz to head the *yeshivah*. Rabbi Shlomo Ephraim was more than fit for the post and a warm exponent of the Maharal's approach. But this only assuaged somewhat the insult that they had paid the Maharal and Rabbi Betzalel.

"Father," Rabbi Betzalel told the Maharal soon after this vote, "I have received an offer to head the *yeshivah* in Kellin.

THE MAHARAL

I think I should go there. Here in Prague there is no future for me."

"Go there, my son," the Maharal replied. "Your mother and I will be sad to be parted from you, but you are right. Hashem has meant for you to teach Torah. Here in Prague you cannot exercise all of your gifts. Here you are unappreciated. Go to Kellin. May you find true happiness and satisfaction there."

Perl cried. She and the Maharal were old now. Would they ever see Betzalel again? And his children? But she too was glad that he was on his way. He was no longer a young man, and it was good that he was fulfilling his great potential.

Rabbi Betzalel and his family moved to Kellin. Rabbi Betzalel promised his old parents that he would write them and visit them quite often.

True to his promise, Rabbi Betzalel wrote regularly to his parents. Then, one week a letter arrived from Kellin written in his wife's handwriting. The Maharal read it, and tears sprung to his eyes. When Perl came into his study, she saw the letter in his hand and the look of grief on his face. "What happened?" she asked in dread, for she already knew the answer in her heart. Betzalel, their beloved and only son, had passed away.

This was a great blow that could not be alleviated.

But even with this tragic news, life continued, and the Maharal's family continued to grow.

The Maharal published one more work, *Ner Mitzvah*, on *Chanukah*. He was to publish nothing else after this.

In the same year, 1600, the Maharal's granddaughter Chavah (daughter of Feigeleh and Rabbi Yitzchak Katz) married Rabbi Shmuel Bacharach, *darshan* of Prague. Chavah was a great source of pride to her grandparents. She was "the mother of all living things in Torah and in good deeds, who never had an equal," as she was described in later years by her

THE MAHARAL

grandson in his introduction to his famous *sefer*, *Chavos Yair*, whose title includes a reference to her name. We learn from this introduction as well that Chavah Bacharach was well-learned. She learned the *Midrash* independently and made critical remarks about the *Matnos Kehunah* (the commentary on the *Midrash*, which was first written and published in her lifetime), and she was an excellent Hebrew stylist.

The son of Rabbi Yitzchak Chayes (the Maharal's departed brother-in-law), Rabbi Manish, who was Chief Rabbi of Vilna, sent the Maharal a warm letter of congratulations and attended the wedding. In this way, Rabbi Manish demonstrated that despite the troubles over the post of Chief Rabbi of Prague, his feelings were warm toward the Maharal and his family.

The Maharal and Perl also had the great pleasure of seeing their offspring attain greatness in Torah and attain important rabbinical posts.

Chaim Kohn, son of Feigeleh, became Chief Rabbi of Nikolsburg, where the Maharal himself had been chief rabbi for nineteen years three decades before.

Moshe, the son of Reichel, became the chief rabbi of various communities. He was a famous *darshan*, known for his expertise both in the revealed Torah and the Kabbalah. Thanks to his wife Sarah, who was an accomplished businesswoman, Rabbi Moshe was quite wealthy.

Then Shmuel, son of Rabbi Betzalel, became the mayor of the Jewish ghetto of Prague. Rabbi Shmuel was very tall and good-looking, and many people remarked that he was the mirror image of the Maharal.

Soon after this, Rabbi Shmuel had a son, whom he named Betzalel after his own departed father. The Maharal dearly loved this small child, his great-grandchild, and he and Perl treated him with unbounded love.

And so the Maharal and his wife inherited the great wealth

of old age, which was to see their children and grandchildren grow and become adults who embodied the values of charity, piety and dedication to the Torah.

28

The Message for Posterity

"BUT, YOUR HIGHNESS—"

"I shall not receive anyone." King Rudolf's face was heavy. "Let the delegation from Vienna wait. Tell them I am engaged."

"Yes, your highness."

"I shall be in my alchemical laboratory from eleven until two with Andreas Hannewaldt. From two to four, I shall be visiting Bartholomaeus Spranger, who is painting a woodland scene for my parlor. I have no interest in these affairs of state. Let them wait."

"Yes, your highness."

It was 1604, and the reign of King Rudolf was beginning to decline slowly, as the increasingly eccentric emperor took greater interest in the arts and the occult than the world of politics, and occasionally lapsed into melancholy.

THE MAHARAL

The king stopped before a portrait of him on the wall and gazed at it appreciatively. Rudolf was portrayed as Vertumnus, the Roman idol of the changing seasons. In the portrait, Rudolf was entirely made up of fruits, vegetables and flowers. His nose was a pear, his eyebrows stalks of wheat, his eyes nuts, his mouth cherries and other fruits, his forehead the butt of a squash, his hair a wild conglomeration of wheat stalks, grape clusters and fruits. His beard consisted of berries and plums, his neck of beets and cucumbers, and flowers graced his mantle, composed of great squashes. Rudolf almost smiled, and he went on.

It took some days before a petition from the Jews of Prague came before the king. King Rudolf read it hurriedly. It was no concern of his, absolutely of no interest. "The Chief Rabbi, Loew son of Betzalel, is old and sick, and needs to rest. He has himself requested that he be freed from this office."

Rabbi Loew! Yes, he was that rabbi of the Jews who was so well-versed in the occult arts. A pity he was ill. But everyone was getting older, the empire was only getting more corrupt and, matters were going from bad to worse. This was a sign of the times. Well, he was sorry to hear that the rabbi was no longer well. That was a man for whom he could have respect, not the breed of the new generation that swarmed about him now. The old order had come to an end, and had been replaced with confusion.

And what was this? The petition continued, "We ask to be allowed to employ in his place as the next Chief Rabbi, Rabbi Shlomo Ephraim. He has this to recommend him, that he has no relatives in the community, being of Luntschitz, and thus his judgments are sure to be impartial."

King Rudolf could read between the lines. He had heard of nepotism in the Jewish community of Prague. Father appointed son, brother-in-law recompensed brother-in-law, and decisions were made not on the basis of what is right but on the basis of which relative might benefit. Was Rudolf's jaded reading of the petition accurate? Or was it only his melancholy imagining of what was in reality not there?

Rudolf shook his head. Everywhere was corruption, intrigue and in-fighting. It wasn't his concern. But would the new Chief Rabbi be a leader that the government could deal with? Rudolf turned to the man who stood waiting before him with flat and venal eyes.

"What do you say, Lang?" asked Rudolf.

"The commended appointment seems quite creditable, my lord." Philip Lang had in the last few years taken advantage of Rudolf's passivity to become his evil genius, ruling to some degree and monitoring all of the king's correspondence.

"Very well," declared the king, and scrawled his name at the bottom of the petition: Approved.

The Talmud says, "Who are the kings? The rabbis."

A king very different from Rudolf sat in the dark within his inner chamber. The Maharal's tall frame was now bent over, and his face wrinkled and weary. He was ninety-two years old and ailing, and he could no longer rule over Prague and Bohemia. A new generation of Torah scholars was growing. He was glad to see that Rabbi Shlomo Ephraim would be taking his place, the man who had four years previously taken charge of the *beis midrash*. He was a man who had acquired Torah in all forty-eight ways required by the *Mishnah*, and he would make a fine leader for Prague.

There was a sound of footsteps. Perl opened the door, her face illuminated by the candlestick she held.

"You're sitting in the dark!" she exclaimed.

"Yes, I was reviewing my learning and the candle burned out."

Perl laughed. "So you continued to review by heart. Let me get you a candle anyway." She placed a fresh candle in the candle-holder upon the Maharal's desk and lit it. "Rabbi

THE MAHARAL

Shlomo Ephraim has come to visit you. Shall I let him in?"

"I'll see him." The Maharal rose.

"No, don't trouble yourself."

"I'd like to sit with him on the balcony."

The Maharal went out to the balcony, and Rabbi Shlomo Ephraim soon joined him. In the dusky garden, the yellow-green luminescence of the fireflies winked. Grape leaves and bunches of grapes were draped next to trees laden with ripened purple plums, green figs and blushing apricots, and sprays of mint, sage and thyme framed a quaint path paved with white limestone.

The two men sat in comfortable silence for some time, and then Rabbi Shlomo Ephraim spoke. "How sad that there is still so much wrangling. A child takes twenty years to mature. Yet the Jewish nation has grown for so many centuries and suffered so many lessons of exile, and still we prefer the pleasure of fighting to the happiness of harmony."

"You are quite right," the Maharal replied. "In fact, fighting and dissension, one Jew not loving another—these things are the very essence of what exile is. But when Jews join together in love, that itself marks the beginning of our redemption."

The Maharal had been inspired to speak, and he thoughtfully went on talking.

"The exile cannot last forever, because exile is something unnatural. Hashem made a natural order according to which every nation lives upon its own land. We too have our own land: the land of Israel. Our exile from our land is unnatural. This gives us hope, for nothing unnatural can last. Things must ultimately revert to their natural order. And the natural state of the Jews is to live in the land of Israel, under our own rule. (*Netzach Yisrael*)

"Ultimately, Hashem will redeem us. The exile cannot last forever. Even if the Jews do not repent, they will be redeemed.

Hashem did not choose Avraham because of his righteousness. Rather, Hashem was pleased with the essence of Avraham. Similarly, Hashem redeemed the Jews from Egypt even though He knew that they would subsequently sin. This is because Hashem redeems the Jews without looking at their righteousness: He desires the Jews because of what they are in essence. And in the same way that the Jews were redeemed from Egypt, so will they always be redeemed. (*Gevuros Hashem*)

"Then, before *Mashiach* comes, there will be a spiritual decline. Hashem will be very far from the Jews, and the Torah will be forgotten among them. (*Tiferes Yisrael*)

"This is because before *Mashiach* comes and changes reality, the old reality will have to be swept away. Every new level of reality must be preceded by a breakdown in the previous state of reality. As long is there is a preceding reality, the new form cannot take hold, for the first form keeps it from coming. The more radical the new form, the more must it nullify the first form. (*Chiddushei Aggados*)

"When the redemption does come, it shall not be in one quick stage. We have fallen so low, compared to the high level which we will ultimately reach, that Hashem will not redeem us in one stage. But nevertheless, the redemption will be very swift." (*Ohr Chadash*)

"The whole non-Jewish world will be opposed to *Mashiach*. Before he rules, there will be the War of Gog and Magog. All the nations shall rise against *Mashiach*, but he will conquer them and become king over the entire world. Why will this war take place? When *Mashiach* has not yet reached his ultimate level, the nations of the world will have great power as well, and they will want to overcome *Mashiach*. Then *Mashiach* son of Yosef will die, before the ultimate rule of *Mashiach* son of David.

"And then, with the rulership of *Mashiach*, the world will no longer be subject to physical rules. People will be freed of their evil inclination, and all of humanity will turn with one heart to serve Hashem.

"But this period will not last forever. The days of *Mashiach*, at the end of days, will in fact be a short period. It will be followed quickly by the resurrection of the dead and the World-to-Come. It is impossible for a person to rise instantly from the low level of this world to the high level of the resurrection of the dead and the World-to-Come. Therefore, mankind will rise in stages. The first stage up will be the days of *Mashiach*. And afterwards, mankind will rise to the highest level. So the purpose of *Mashiach* is to raise all of existence up from one level to the next, one level at a time." (*Netzach Yisrael*)

The two great Torah leaders sat in silence. If only men could change their hearts, then, as the Talmud states, *Mashiach* and an end to suffering could arrive even now, for nothing else is delaying him.

The two rabbis sat in the darkening evening as though waiting to hear the footsteps of the bearer of glad tidings. And then it grew dark altogether. The moon sank behind a steeple, and they came back into the house.

29

The Final Days

THE MAHARAL'S LAST YEARS WERE PEACEFUL AND GOOD PRAGUE was growing famous as a great city of Torah. A chronicler who visited the city in 1604 wrote, "In Prague, there exists a very famous community whose fragrance is widely spread, a big town, full of wise, learned men, wealthy men, all adorned with the crown of a good reputation. They are distinguished by knowledge of Torah, piety and the fear of Hashem; it is a holy community for which it would be vain to seek an equal and the like of which has seldom been found."

The Maharal basked in the company of his family, and all about him, like olive tree shoots round a table, were his students, rabbis of great renown, were spreading his ideas and his methods, particularly in the area of teaching Torah.

Rabbi Pinchas Halevi Horowitz, husband of the Maharal's granddaughter Shlift, became judge in Prague.

THE MAHARAL

Rabbi Naftali Katz, son of Feigeleh, became *darshan* of Prague.

Then Rabbi Moshe, son of Reichel, also became a *darshan* in Prague.

Rabbi Meir, son of the Maharal's daughter Tillah, became a rabbi in Prague.

And Rabbi Shmuel Bacharach, husband of the Maharal's granddaughter Chavah, became Chief Rabbi of Worms. But this did not last. Sometime later, Rabbi Bacharach passed away, and Chavah was widowed.

And so the quiet years wore on, and in their waning shadow, the Maharal and his wife found peace and light.

But the time came when even the unusually long and productive career of the Maharal could last no longer. . . .

The man on horseback dug his spurs into his horse, and the beleaguered animal, its eyes wild with the effort of the journey, its mouth foaming at the stiffly-held bit, shook its head. But the man was a good rider, and the horse continued cantering up the road.

It was then, when the man came in sight of Prague, that he caught a glimpse of a mass of people in the street. Am I too late then? he thought to himself and forced his laboring animal into a desperate gallop.

Coming into Prague at last, he made his way to the Jewish ghetto, where, as he had glimpsed from afar, a crowd of people filled the streets. The man flung himself from the horse and accosted the first passerby he saw.

"What news? What news?" he demanded, panting from the effort of the mad race.

"Who are you?" the man replied.

"I'm a doctor. I've come to administer to Rabbi Loew!"

The man shook his head, tears rolling softly into his streaky gray beard.

The doctor ran up to the Jews in the crowd. Could it be

that he was too late, that the Maharal had gone to higher realms? But there was no need to ask. The weeping faces, the keening women, the slow progression to the Jewish cemetery, all bore silent testimony.

The Maharal had passed away. It was the eighteenth of Elul, 5369—eighteen, in Hebrew, the symbol of *chai*, life. By the secular calendar it was August 22, 1609. The Maharal had lived to the age of ninety-seven. His had been a long life that had transformed the lives of thousands and tens of thousands, a life whose teachings and inspiration would continue to affect the thought of all branches of Torah until the present day.

The Maharal was the "pillar, strong as metal, on which all Jews rely," wrote Rabbi Yom Tov Heller, author of *Tosafos Yom Tov*.

He was "the leader of the generation, the light of Israel," in the words of the Maharam of Lublin.

In a letter to the Maharal published in *Nesivos Olam*, one of his outstanding students, Rabbi Yisrael, addressed him, "Our righteous *Mashiach* at our head, our king, the king of Yehudah, the extraordinary *gaon*, you are king of Israel and leader of the generation, may you live forever." The hope of the generation had not lived forever. The generation had not merited the blossoming of the buds of redemption and the coming of *Mashiach*.

Those who could begin to appreciate who the Maharal was, and those who only had regarded him with awe; those who had learned his teachings and those who had been touched by his leadership; those who had understood something of his vision, and those who had been awed by his countenance; those whose shirts were ripped in mourning—all knew that a great man had lived and now he lived no more. All knew that an era had passed, defined by the greatness of the man who had lived in it, who had thought and spoken, written and created insights into Torah that would deepen and broaden men's minds for the centuries to come.

The doctor pushed his way through the throng of mourners. There, surrounded by the leading rabbis, surrounded by the family of the Maharal, on the shoulders of ten black-robed men, was the long, unvarnished wooden casket of the Maharal, held motionless as a rabbi eulogized him in a sobbing voice. The doctor could barely make out the words; his eyes were fixed on the casket.

Why was he so fascinated? The casket held only his body. And yet the spirit of the Maharal hung about it still. It was a place to focus on, because it was the last grasp that the people would ever have upon the Maharal himself. Soon his holy body would be buried in the crowded Jewish cemetery in Prague, and they would have only his memory, his books, his teachings. But here was the Maharal himself, in a sense, and that drew and fascinated the doctor. Here, in the midst of death, he yet felt the overwhelming presence of life.

Winter passed and spring arrived in the land. The time of the songbird arrived, and the voice of the turtledove was heard. The date tree ripened and the grapes wafted their scent. Perl could not live long without the Maharal, for they had been as one. Together, they had been the center of the lives of their children, grandchildren, great-grandchildren and sons- and daughters-in-law. And the Maharal had in turn been the center of his wife's life. Wherever he had gone, whatever he had decided to do, she had gone along with him and accommodated him.

Now she was alone on this earth and aging. Yes, she was surrounded by her loving family, but she was an old woman. Hers had been a life of modesty and dedication to Torah. Her husband had written, "The World-to-Come is non-physical. So it is fit only for a person who is modest and steeped in Torah, for such a person is spiritual." (*Chiddushei Aggados*) All her life, Perl had lived a life dedicated to goodness and to matters of the spirit. Courageous and active when she had to be, as when she had many years earlier confronted the mounted soldier who had attempted to rob her, retiring and reserved when that was appropriate.

Half a year passed, and on the tenth of *Iyar*, Perl, the Maharal's widow, passed away. She had lived to ninety-four.

The sun had set, and now the moon as well had sunken, and the earth was darkened.

But the children of the Maharal continued their own lives.

The Maharal's great-granddaughter (the granddaughter of Betzalel and daughter of Shmuel) married her father's cousin, the Maharal's grandson Chaim (son of Feigeleh). Rabbi Chaim became the head of the *yeshivah* in Prague.

Soon afterwards, the second daughter of Shmuel married Rabbi Yaakov, Chief Rabbi of Hessin.

Naftali, the second son of Feigeleh, became Chief Rabbi of Prossnitz.

Then Gitteleh had a third son, whom she named Betzalel.

Some years had passed since the Maharal's granddaughter Chavah had been widowed. Now she received an offer of marriage from Rabbi Yeshayah Horowitz, author of *Shnei Luchos Habris*. One of the most outstanding rabbis of the last few centuries, he was on his way to the land of Israel. But Chavah's answer was negative. In honor of her departed husband, she did not feel it right to do so.

Many years later, in 1650, Chavah herself set out for the Holy Land, but she passed away while still in the midst of her travels, in Sofia (in Bulgaria).

According to Rabbi Meir Perles' *Megillas Yuchasin*, the Maharal was known to have committed a miracle from the world of truth many years after his passing away. And this is the story that is recorded:

The Maharal had acquired three burial places next to each

THE MAHARAL

other in Prague's Jewish cemetery, for himself, for his wife and for his son Betzalel. But Betzalel had died in Kellin in 1600, and so he had been buried there. In consequence, the Maharal promised Betzalel's son Shmuel that he would get that burial spot.

It was 1654, and Rabbi Shmuel was dying. When the *chevrah kaddisha* came to speak with him, he told them that his grandfather, the Maharal, had promised him that he could be buried in the spot next to him.

The members of the *chevrah kaddisha* explained that it would no longer be possible. In the many years since the Maharal had passed away, new graves had been dug so near the Maharal's grave that there was now only a very narrow space next to the Maharal, too narrow to fit the body of Rabbi Shmuel.

Rabbi Shmuel replied, "I want you to go and dig the grave now, even while I am alive. If you see that there is not enough room for me to fit, ask my grandfather's pardon and request that he move aside so that there will be enough room for me to be buried next to him, as he had promised me."

The members of the *chevrah kaddisha* complied with this request. When they asked the Maharal to kindly move himself over to make room for his grandson, his tombstone moved over, and the space of the newly-dug grave was broadened, so that there was enough room to bury the body of Rabbi Shmuel.

After Rabbi Shmuel passed away, he was buried in that spot. Immediately afterwards, the Maharal's grave shifted over, and Rabbi Shmuel's gravesite again became a narrow strip of land. There was no room for a normal-sized headstone to be set up, and so instead, a tall and narrow headstone was fit into the thin spot.

This was recorded in the records of the *chevrah kaddisha*, which were burned in the fire of 1689. Nevertheless, the headstone is there to see, and the story was well-known to all the members of the community and to the Maharal's offspring.

30

The Maharal's Legacy

SOME GREAT TEACHERS IN TORAH LEAVE BEHIND SCHOOLS OR MOVEments. But others are individuals who do not leave behind such vessels for others to fill. Such teachers leave behind great inspiration but not an organized movement. The Maharal was apparently the second type of teacher.

But his writings were read and passed on throughout the years.

One of the great sages of this century proclaimed, "The Maharal was the father of the approach of the Vilna Gaon on the one hand and, on the other, of *chassidism*."

In the early eighteen hundreds, the Maharal was acclaimed as one of the great inspirations of Polish *chassidism*, in particular of the schools of Pshishcha and Kotzk (which stemmed from the Chozeh of Lublin's student, Rabbi Yaakov Yitzchak, (Der Yid Hakadosh, 1765-1827). His writings were

THE MAHARAL

celebrated by Rabbi Simchah Bunim of Pshishcha (1759–1827) and Rabbi Menachem Mendel of Kotzk (1787–1858). These great teachers found deep inspiration in the teachings of the Maharal and directed that his hard-to-find writings should be reprinted. Once, when Rabbi Menachem Mendel of Kotzk's son-in-law grew ill, Rabbi Avraham of Sochatchov sent someone to pray at the side of the Maharal's grave, and he directed the man to tell the Maharal that at the time that Rabbi Menachem Mendel of Kotzk reprinted the Maharal's *sefarim*, he made the learning of those *sefarim* obligatory upon every *chassid*. Rabbi Menachem Mendel of Kotzk went as far as to tell one of his students, Rabbi Nachum Yisrael of Lifna, to set aside his *chassidic sefarim* and learn only the Maharal.

In addition, the father of the Rebbe of Sochatchov once said that the Maharal of Prague had intelligence even in his feet.

The Maharal's influence is also seen in the teachings of Rabbi Shneur Zalman, founder of Chabad *chassidism*.

In more recent generations, there have been others who have turned to the Maharal and made him one of the cornerstones of their teaching. Rabbi Yitzchak Hutner, the *rosh yeshivah* of Yeshivas Rabbeinu Chaim Berlin, often referred to and was inspired by the Maharal's wisdom.

Rabbi Eliyahu Dessler, the author of *Michtav Me'eliyahu*, made extensive use of the works of the Maharal, taught his students how to study the Maharal and encouraged the production of a revised and corrected edition of his works.

Although the Maharal was active four hundred years ago, he is very much alive in the world of Torah thought and insight. The Talmud says that a *tzaddik* is alive even after his death. Life is not the body but the mind and soul. Even on the most simple level, the Maharal is with us in his *sefarim* and in the great Torah leaders, down to our generation, who have been inspired by him and who, blazing their own paths, have made Torah a new and engaging challenge.

Torah constitutes a means of perfecting character and of serving Hashem with complete truth. For those who recognize that, the teachings of a profound and original thinker, whose teachings glow with a healthy spirituality, love of Hashem and love of the Jewish people, are a necessary balm to their spirit and refreshing waters to their soul.

Such were the teachings of the Maharal, teachings that present the balanced confluence of the human mind and divine wisdom.